Praise for *The Bogleheads' Guide to the Three-Fund Portfolio*

"Forget picking individual stocks. Stop hunting for star money managers. Don't bother guessing the market's direction. All this is nonsense that'll enrich Wall Street at your expense. Instead, listen to Taylor Larimore, buy three total market index funds—and put yourself on the far surer road to financial success."

— Jonathan Clements, founder of HumbleDollar.com and author of *From Here to Financial Happiness*

"The vast majority of investment products and services are over-wrought and cost too much, but the Bogleheads are here to say that it doesn't have to be that way. In this single, easy-to-digest volume, lead Boglehead Taylor Larimore shares how three low-cost mutual funds are all you really need for a successful investing life, whether you're just starting out or have been a serious investor for years. 'The majesty of simplicity' have long been Taylor's watchwords; this book is the embodiment of those virtues."

— Christine Benz, senior columnist, Morningstar, Inc., and author of *30-Minute Money Solutions: A Step-by-Step Guide to Managing Your Finances*

"Usually if it's too good to be true, it is. Taylor's investment strategy is an exception to the rule. Most investors will be far better off if they follow Taylor's simple, yet sophisticated strategy. It will have a profound impact on their lives."

— George U. "Gus" Sauter, Chief Investment Officer, Vanguard (retired)

The Bogleheads'

Guide to the Three-Fund Portfolio

How a Simple Portfolio of Three Total Market Index Funds Outperforms Most Investors with Less Risk

Taylor Larimore

WILEY

For general information on our other products and services or for technical support, please contact our Customer Care Department within the United States at (800) 762-2974, outside the United States at (317) 572-3993, or fax (317) 572-4002.

Wiley publishes in a variety of print and electronic formats and by print-on-demand. Some material included with standard print versions of this book may not be included in e-books or in print-on-demand. If this book refers to media such as a CD or DVD that is not included in the version you purchased, you may download this material at http://booksupport.wiley.com. For more information about Wiley products, visit www.wiley.com.

Library of Congress Cataloging-in-Publication Data:

Names: Larimore, Taylor, 1924– author.
Title: The Bogleheads' guide to the three-fund portfolio : how a simple
   portfolio of three total market index funds outperforms most investors
   with less risk / by Taylor Larimore.
Description: Hoboken, New Jersey : John Wiley & Sons, Inc., [2018] | Includes
   index. |
Identifiers: LCCN 2018009787 (print) | LCCN 2018011286 (ebook) | ISBN
   978-1-119-48737-1 (pdf) | ISBN 978-1-119-48735-7 (epub) | ISBN 978-1-119-48733-3
   (cloth)
Subjects: LCSH: Investments. | Portfolio management. | Bogle, John C.
Classification: LCC HG4521 (ebook) | LCC HG4521 .L3195 2018 (print) | DDC
   332.63/27–dc23
LC record available at https://lccn.loc.gov/2018009787

Printed in the United States of America
10 9 8 7 6 5 4 3 2 1

To Patricia Steckman Larimore, my beloved wife during our 62 years together,

and

Taffy Gould, who now shares my golden years with me,

and

John C. Bogle, who created the three total market index funds

that made The Three-Fund Portfolio possible

The author is donating all royalties to The John C. Bogle
Center for Financial Literacy

Contents

Foreword

There is something truly remarkable about the intersection of something old and something new. First, a World War II veteran of the Battle of the Bulge has an idea for building a better world for investors. A decade later, modern technology begins to create unprecedented opportunities for the development of social networks, opening a whole new world for interpersonal communication. That combination of man and technology led to the creation of an investor-driven website for individual investors.

The Army combat veteran, born in 1924, is Taylor Larimore, distinguished citizen of Miami, Florida, and a truly wonderful human being. The new technology is the Internet. The idea: to allow investors in the Vanguard mutual funds to share their ideas, their investment experiences, and their financial strategies with one another, as it is said, "without fear or favor."

Founded by Taylor in 1998 as the "Vanguard Diehards," the name of the new website was changed to the "Bogleheads" in 2007. Their first meeting—Diehards I—took place in March 2000, when I joined some 20 Vanguard investors in Taylor's Miami condominium for dinner, friendship, and lively conversation about investment strategy and policy.

Then to Vanguard's home in Valley Forge, Pennsylvania, on June 8, 2001, with 40 Bogleheads in attendance. Then to Chicago, where Morningstar hosted the three-day gathering for 50 dedicated investors. Next, to Denver and the Chartered Financial Analysts Conference in 2004, with 90 Bogleheads in attendance.

On to San Diego 2008, and to Fort Worth in 2009, before settling down to roost each year thereafter at a mid-size hotel near

Vanguard's headquarters in the Philadelphia region. The hotel's capacity limits the attendance to some 225 Bogleheads and the openings are quickly filled—a full house every year since then.

I've talked to the Bogleheads at all of these meetings. Each October, for ten years now, I'm asked to summarize the major events at Vanguard, in the mutual fund industry, and in the financial markets, and to place them in historical perspective. (The format has barely changed.)

Taylor Larimore is known unofficially as "the King of the Bogleheads"; his friend Mel Lindauer is known as "the Prince." Mel runs these annual gatherings, at which a range of experts speak, including authors (and investment advisors), Bill Bernstein and Rick Ferri. In recent years, Gus Sauter, former Chief Investment Officer at Vanguard, now retired, has become a regular speaker.

But the limited size and scope of these gatherings merely scratches the surface of the vast network the Bogleheads have developed. To date, the Bogleheads.org forum has been receiving up to 4.5 million hits per day, and in a single day the site has been visited by as many as 90,000 unique individuals. I believe the forum is the most popular financial website in America.

And why not? The members want to help one another. There are no financial incentives for doing so, nor are there any costs for participating. "Selfless" is the *modus operandi*.

THE THREE-FUND PORTFOLIO

Taylor Larimore has participated in the writing and publication of two earlier books, both reaching large numbers of investors: *The Bogleheads' Guide to Investing* (2006) and *The Bogleheads' Guide to Retirement Planning* (2009). In *The Bogleheads' Guide to the Three-Fund Portfolio*, Taylor goes on his own to explore one of the subjects dearest to his heart—using three all-market index funds: Vanguard Total Stock Market Index Fund (U.S. stock market), Vanguard Total International Stock Index Fund (non-U.S. stock market), and Vanguard Total Bond Market Index Fund (U.S. bonds).

Taylor's idea combines the nth degree of diversification, a sensible investment balance between stocks and bonds, efficiency, and economy. "Simplicity" is the watchword. Yes, as he notes, investors' allocation among these three asset classes depends on their particular investment goals, risk tolerance, age, and wealth. Even investors' temperament comes into play, for financial markets are volatile. Sometimes the financial markets giveth, and sometimes (with far less frequency) they taketh away.

I'd estimate that thousands of Vanguard investors have subscribed to the idea of "The Three-Fund Portfolio." As originally conceived by Taylor, the initial allocation into each of the three index funds would be based on the investor's goals, time frame, risk tolerance and personal financial situation.

A WORD ABOUT NON-U.S. STOCKS

In my first book, *Bogle on Mutual Funds*, published in 1994, I wrote that a long-term investor need not allocate any of his or her assets to non-U.S. stocks. But if they disagreed, I argued, they should limit their holdings to 20% of their stock portion, given the significant extra risks involved (such as currency risk and sovereign risk).

My opinion was based on my expectation that the American economy would continue to grow over the long term, and that the market values of U.S. corporations would grow faster than the values of non-U.S. corporations. Since 1994, as it was to happen, the U.S. S&P 500 Index was to rise by 743%, while the EAFE (Europe, Australasia, and Far East) Index of non-U.S. stocks rose by 237%.

That I was right is beside the point. It may have been luck. But now that U.S. stocks have dominated for nearly 25 years, it may well be time for reversion to the mean, with non-U.S. stocks leading the way rather than following. Who really knows? No one knows what tomorrow may bring. But I'm inclined to stick by my earlier conclusion that holdings of non-U.S. stocks should be limited to no more than 20% of equities.

For U.S. investors, Taylor suggests that 20% of the equity allocation should be placed in a Total International Stock Index Fund. That suggested 20% is essentially a compromise between my suggested maximum of 20% and the minimum 20% recommended by a Vanguard study.

A GOOD BOOK BY A WISE AUTHOR

Please note that the fine points of asset allocation in The Three-Fund Portfolio constitute only a small part of this fine book. It is replete with sound advice and will effectively serve both experienced and novice investors. Taylor describes the investment lessons he learned the hard way—by risking his own hard-earned money and falling short of the market's return. He tried to beat the market by picking individual stocks, both through an investment club and on his own; he chased the returns of hot mutual funds, only to suffer the inevitable fate of reversion to the mean; he followed investment newsletters that claimed to be able to beat the market, but, of course, did not; he invested with a stock broker who was good at collecting fees, but had no ability to beat the market.

Finally, Taylor read my first book, *Bogle on Mutual Funds*, and was persuaded by my unassailable Cost Matters Hypothesis: The gross return of the market, minus the costs of investing, equals net return to investors. If active investors in aggregate own the market, which they do, as a group they receive the market's return minus the high costs of active investing. Index investors also own the market, but at rock-bottom cost. So the average actively-managed portfolio will, of necessity, underperform the average indexed portfolio. Investing in index funds is the only way to guarantee that you'll receive your fair share of the market's return.

Taylor goes on to list many of the other benefits of broad-market indexing, including the elimination of manager risk, individual stock risk, sector risk, and tracking error, just to name a few. He cites numerous experts who support index investing, such as David Swensen, Warren Buffett, and Paul Samuelson. Nobel laureate William Sharpe concluded his influential paper, "The Arithmetic of Active Management," with these words: "Properly measured, the average actively-managed dollar must underperform the average passively-managed dollar, net of costs. Empirical analyses that appear to refute this principle are guilty of improper measurement."

The Three-Fund Portfolio will help you to develop a sound asset allocation strategy, make smart investment selections, and guide the implementation of your plan. Taylor offers one final piece of advice, and it's a mantra I've repeated countless times throughout my long career in finance: *Stay the course.* As I said in my book *Common Sense on Mutual Funds*, "No matter what happens, stick to your program. I've said, 'Stay the course' a thousand times, and I meant it every time. It's the most important single piece of investment wisdom I can give to you."

"A POWER SEEN FROM AFAR"

In writing the Foreword to *The Bogleheads' Guide to Investing* in 2005, I cited this expression from *Democracy in America*, written by Alexis de Tocqueville in 1835, nearly two centuries ago.

> As soon as several of the inhabitants of the United States have taken up an opinion or a feeling they wish to promote, they look out for mutual assistance, and as soon as they have found one another out, they combine. From that moment they are no longer isolated men, but *a power seen from afar*, whose actions serve for an example and whose language is listened to. [Italics mine.]

Yes, with Taylor Larimore's leadership, the Bogleheads have become a power in the field of independent, unbiased investment information. Be sure to visit the remarkable Bogleheads.org website. Test your investment decisions on the anvil of the ideas offered by the intelligent investors who frequent the site and are eager to serve you. You'll find a family of fellow investors who believe in my rock-solid philosophy of long-term investing focused largely on broad- market, low-cost index funds. When joining the forum, you can exchange your own ideas with those of other investors who have had experience with their own asset allocations, as well as with many other issues.

Index funds are designed simply to assure you that you will earn your fair share of the returns delivered in each segment of The Three-Fund Portfolio—or any other indexing strategy that meets your needs. Enjoy Taylor's wonderful book, learn about the benefits of index funds, and reap the benefits of low-cost investing. There will be times when the waters are rough, and fear, even panic, will hold sway. When those trying times come, be sure to, yes, **Stay the course**!

John C. Bogle
September 21, 2017

Preface

The History of the Bogleheads' Three-Fund Portfolio

I often am asked, "What's so special about the Three-Fund Portfolio?"

The answer is simple: By owning just three low-cost total market index funds (Total U.S. Equity, Total U.S. Bond, and Total International Equity), investors have historically outperformed the vast majority of mutual funds over time.

I'll start at the beginning and will attempt to share with you some of the lessons I learned the hard way, over many, many years. Yes, I, a nonagenarian, have seen just about everything the world has to share.

The Roaring Twenties were marked by great exuberance in the stock market. The Dow Industrials climbed from a low of 66 in 1920 to a high of 381 in 1929. Then came the worst Bear Market in U.S. history. The Dow plunged 89% to a low of 41 in 1932. (An 89% decline requires a 909% gain to recover.) A Bear Market in stocks can be a terrifying experience if your financial future is at stake.

I was born in 1924, the year the first open-end mutual fund was established (Massachusetts Investment Trust). The closest equivalents were called "investment trusts." In 1929, my grandfather, Christopher Coombs, was one of three principals at the top of the world's largest investment trust—United Founders Corporation. Investment trusts, later called "mutual funds," must be in my blood.

The year 1929 was the beginning of a long and terrible depression in the United States. Unemployment rose from 3% to 25% of the nation's workforce. More than 8,500 U.S. banks failed. There was no government insurance, as now provided by the Federal Deposit Insurance Corporation (FDIC), which insures most deposits to $250,000 in insured banks. During that horrible time, many bank depositors lost their life savings.

My parents owned a restaurant on the outskirts of Boston. As the depression deepened, few people could afford to eat out. With fewer and fewer customers, my parents lost the business. Having no other income (Social Security and Unemployment Compensation didn't exist at that time), our family left Boston and moved into my grandfather's waterfront winter mansion in Miami. A few years later, Grandfather and his United Founders Corporation went bankrupt. His home was sold on the courthouse steps, and we were forced to move into a small Miami apartment. It was an unexpected shock for all of us.

This was my personal introduction to the stock market.

Lesson learned: A 100% stock portfolio can be dangerous.

After returning from World War II and graduating from the University of Miami, I began selling life insurance. I was the leading first-year agent for the Mutual Benefit Life Insurance Company, and I was just beginning to earn serious money. Despite my wariness of stocks, I joined with other friends to become a member of a newly formed stock investment club, organized by a neighbor who was a Bache & Co. stock broker. The idea was that each member would contribute $50 per month to buy individual stocks, carefully selected by our own revolving three-person Investment Committee.

Our club members started out with great optimism, encouraged by the Bache broker, who soon became our "friend." (I didn't know then that every good salesman tries to become your friend.) Unfortunately, our investment club's stock-picking ability was less than stellar, and despite our careful analysis, we eventually realized that our stock returns (after hidden brokerage costs) were substantially underperforming the overall stock market. This ended our investment club experiment.

This was my personal introduction to stock-picking.

Lesson learned: Believing a broker is your friend can be dangerous.

When the club disbanded, I continued to buy individual stocks, thinking I could do better. After a few more years, it became evident that I was even worse at picking stocks than our investment committee had been. Fortunately, this ended my attempts to beat the market by buying individual stocks.

There's no way that spending a few hours a week looking at individual securities is going to equip an investor to compete with the incredibly talented, highly qualified, extremely-educated individuals who spend their entire professional career trying to pick stocks.

—David Swensen, Chief Investment Officer, Yale University

Lesson learned: Avoid the lure of individual stocks.

My failure to invest successfully in individual stocks made me more determined to find a better way. I began taking regular trips to the library to learn how to "beat the market."

The library subscribed to dozens of financial newsletters. The most popular newsletter at the time was a bi-weekly, *The Mutual Fund Forecaster*, which listed hundreds of mutual funds and showed their past performance over various time periods. The *Forecaster* would recommend which funds to buy (the best performers) and which to sell (the worst performers). I was sold on the idea because the strategy sounded so logical. I bought my own subscription, began buying mutual funds, and dutifully followed the *Forecaster's* recommendations for several years. You can guess what happened.

Our portfolio continued to underperform the market and the *Forecaster* newsletter eventually failed.

Lesson learned: Past performance does not forecast future performance.

Most financial newsletters are written by market timers who believe (or pretend they know) they can forecast Bull and Bear Markets. *All* market-timing letters claim great forecasting ability, usually by showing selected periods when the writer's forecast proved to be correct. I decided to give market timing a try, and for several years I followed the forecasting advice offered by various market-timing newsletters. As you can probably guess again, my results were not good. The funds I bought often underperformed the market, and the funds I sold often did better.

After nearly 50 years in this business, I do not know of anybody who has done market timing successfully and consistently. I don't even know anybody who knows anybody who has done it successfully and consistently.

—Jack Bogle

Lesson learned: Investment newsletters are a waste of money and market timing doesn't work.

Still undaunted, my next attempt to "beat the market" was to study the huge Morningstar Mutual Funds binder. It was six inches thick and updated biweekly. The binder was available in most large libraries, but it's no longer published in print.

Studying the past performance of mutual funds, I learned that Morningstar's top performing 5-Star funds seldom remained at 5 Stars. Many of the top performers became bottom dwellers. That's known as "reversion to the mean." In the investment world, it's the equivalent of gravity—in time, Newton's high-flying stock or stock mutual fund will fall. This was eye-opening to me because, after reading all the mutual fund rankings in most newspapers and magazines, I thought all I had to do was buy the top-performing mutual funds to "beat the market." What else could these rankings be good for? (Answer: to sell newspapers and magazines.)

In 2002, while Jack Bogle was putting the final touches on a speech, "The Telltale Chart," that he was to make at the Morningstar Investment Conference in Chicago, I took the empty seat beside him. In this keynote speech, accompanied by lots of charts, Jack talked about reversion to the mean and much more. His speech helped those in attendance become better investors—and it can help you, too. You may read that speech by using the link below:

https://www.vanguard.com/bogle_site/sp20020626.html.

Buying funds based purely on their past performance is one of the stupidest things an investor can do.

—Jason Zweig, author and *Wall Street Journal* columnist

Lesson learned (again): Past performance does not forecast future performance.

In 1986, we moved our family securities from Merrill Lynch to Vanguard. It was a very difficult decision because our broker was a long-time friend who sometimes invited us to go sailing on his beautiful sailboat (which I now realize we helped pay for).[1] After we left Merrill Lynch, our broker never invited us to go sailing again.

Looking back, leaving Merrill Lynch and moving to Vanguard was the best financial decision we ever made.

Lesson learned: Avoid expensive stock brokers and their hidden fees.

Thinking I could beat the market with Vanguard's no-load funds and their low expense ratios, we accumulated 16 Vanguard funds (mostly actively-managed funds) that were doing well at the time. When one of our funds underperformed, I would replace it with a better-performing fund. I didn't realize it at the time, but I was buying high and selling low. Needless to say, our portfolio continued to underperform the market.

Lesson learned: Buying high and selling low is a losing strategy.

In 1994, I had the good fortune to read Professor Burton Malkiel's, *A Random Walk Down Wall Street* and John Bogle's first book, *Bogle on Mutual Funds*. Suddenly, a light switch turned on. These two books changed everything I thought I knew about investing. Based on academic studies, they both helped convince this writer to become an indexer. ("Indexing" means owning all the stocks in a certain category, as opposed to picking and choosing individual stocks.)

I now own and have read every book written by Mr. Bogle. I credit Jack with leading me to The Three-Fund Portfolio and a comfortable retirement. I enjoy telling my friends, "I live in the house that Jack built!" and I know many friends and Bogleheads who will make the same sorts of claims. Here's what we do, by following the simple Boglehead Investment Philosophy:

---

[1] As it turns out, we were not alone. You may enjoy reading *Where Are All the Customers? Or A Good Hard Look at Wall Street* by Fred Schwed, Jr.; the Wiley Classics edition (2006) is introduced by Jason Zweig.

THE BOGLEHEAD INVESTMENT PHILOSOPHY

1. Develop a workable plan.
2. Invest early and often.
3. Never bear too much or too little risk.
4. Diversify.
5. Never try to time the market.
6. Use index funds when possible.
7. Keep costs low.
8. Minimize taxes.
9. Invest with simplicity.
10. Stay the course.

Bogleheads Speak Out

"Taylor, your posts and additional reading at the start of my investing career convinced me of the wisdom of the three fund portfolio. It has served my family well and has freed up time and energy for the more important things in life."

—EM

"Your original post on the 3total market fund portfolio on the Vanguard Diehards M* [Morningstar] forum in 1999 set me on my investment journey, and a life lesson on simplicity. I'll be indebted to you forever for all your guidance all these years."

—SU

"The older I get, the more I am convinced The Three-Fund Portfolio is an excellent choice for most investors."

—AB

"The best reason I've found to stick to a three-fund portfolio (or close to it): Experience. It took us 30 years or so to learn the value of simplicity. These days we don't stray too far from the basics—Total Stock Market, Total international & Total Bond. (I must say, it sure feels like a big weight has been taken off our backs!)"

—BT

"Thanks to you and the Bogleheads Philosophy, my investing in the 3-Fund Portfolio with a 50/50 asset allocation has been one of the best things I ever did."

—UL

As Easy as 1-2-3: Simple, but not Simplistic

Simple minds think alike, and perhaps there is greatness in vast numbers of them far sharper than my own. But remember, "simple" does not mean "simplistic." To wit: Dow Jones MarketWatch columnist Paul B. Farrell has shared data on eight winning portfolios for investors, which he dubs the "Lazy Portfolios." Included are suggested portfolios from investment luminaries like David Swensen, CIO of the Yale University Endowment; Ted Aronson, founder of $25 billion asset manager AJO Partners; Coffeehouse Investor Bill Schultheis; and bestselling personal investment authors Scott Burns and Bill Bernstein.

Of great interest is that the simplest of them all is the Second Grader Portfolio, a three-fund starter portfolio for young investors like Kevin Roth, the son of financial advisor Allan Roth. Allan Roth is the founder of Wealth Logic and a columnist and author. Together, father and son coauthored, *How a Second Grader Beats Wall Street*, when Kevin was just eight.

Over the last 12 years, the father-son team's investment returns with the three-fund solution (that all Bogleheads know) might surprise you. Admittedly, the portfolio is allocated aggressively toward stocks, consistent with the way young investors with a long life ahead of them should invest. But hard data shows that *simple* wins, as does starting early, like Kevin. Here are the results, published in January 2017 by MarketWatch:

TOTAL RETURNS FOR EIGHT LAZY PORTFOLIOS

PORTFOLIO	1-YEAR RETURN	3-YEAR ANNUAL RETURNS	5-YEAR ANNUAL RETURNS	10-YEAR ANNUAL RETURNS
Aronson Family Taxable	20.16%	8.85%	8.76%	6.77%
Fundadvice Ultimate Buy & Hold	14.73%	6.31%	6.47%	5.09%
Dr. Bernstein's Smart Money	14.11%	7.35%	8.09%	6.17%
Coffeehouse	12.41%	6.68%	8.13%	6.76%
Yale U's Unconventional	14.68%	6.39%	8.05%	6.72%
Dr. Bernstein's No Brainer	20.00%	9.07%	9.88%	7.04%
Margaritaville	19.39%	8.36%	7.74%	5.58%
Second Grader's Starter	24.92%	11.33%	11.77%	7.55%
S&P 500	26.64%	13.97%	15.98%	10.16%

Source: https://www.marketwatch.com/lazyportfolio

"Whether or not an investment portfolio is working for the investor typically rests with its level of complexity," notes Allan Roth. "Some of the worst portfolios I've seen have been so mind-numbingly complex that the investors had no idea what strategy, if any, they were following to achieve such horrible performance. My investing ideology has always been that simple portfolios are better, and I'm not alone in that belief."

Allan and I think alike. Pick a stock/bond allocation that aligns with your goals and have the discipline to accept the bumpy ride the stock market sometimes serves up. (This will show you your "risk tolerance"). No need to buy high and sell low and become your own worst enemy. Like me, like Kevin, like everyone else, you'll find it much easier to stick with your investment plan—tweaking the allocations to the three funds—as you get older.

Source: Allan Roth, "Investing Should Be Simple: A Three-Fund Portfolio Is All You Need," AARP, November 3, 2016

Acknowledgments

No one writes a book by himself. I have read hundreds of books, thousands of articles, and tens of thousands of posts on the Morningstar and Bogleheads online investing forums. I have also watched numerous videos and broadcast interviews. In this book, I'll share with you the summation of what I've learned from all these sources, along with the trial-and-error investment wisdom and perspective that come from both 94 years on this planet and some hard knocks.

I shall be eternally grateful to Taffy Gould, Mel Lindauer and my son, Michael Larimore, for their help in editing and handling all the computer work. Mel was my co-author on two previous *Bogleheads'* books, and his advice has been invaluable as I prepared this third book in our *Bogleheads'* series.

Finally, I want to express my sincere thanks and gratitude to Bill Falloon, Executive Editor, Finance and Investment, at John Wiley & Sons, who worked so diligently and effectively to make this book a worthy addition to the *Bogleheads'* series.

CHAPTER ONE

The Investment Industry

The U.S. investment industry is the largest and most profitable in the world. A 2013 study by the United States Consumer Financial Protection Bureau reported the following: "The total amount spent annually by financial institutions and other financial service providers on consumer financial products and services, including both awareness advertising and direct marketing, is approximately *seventeen billion dollars*." (Italics mine.) This money comes out of the pockets of the industry's customers and goes into the pockets of company owners, brokers, financial advisors and others seeking to make a profit at the expense of investors.

Rick Ferri, CFA, a former stock broker, retired financial advisor, and author of eight financial books, wrote: "Let's face it: Most investment companies are in business to make money *from* you, not *for* you. Every dollar you save in commissions and fee expenses goes right to your bottom line."

Just as the gambling industry wants people to think they can beat the casino, the investment industry wants investors to think they can beat the market. Of course, a few lucky gamblers do beat the casino, but MOST DON'T. It is the same for investors: Some will beat the market, but MOST WON'T.

Why do some investors outperform the market while others don't? Princeton professor Burton G. Malkiel, who co-inspired my "light switch on" moment, mentioned in the Preface, with my reading of his timeless, *A Random Walk Down Wall Street*, offers this explanation: "A blindfolded monkey throwing darts at a newspaper's financial pages could select a portfolio that would do just as well as one carefully selected by experts."

This, of course, means that in a room full of monkeys, as in a room full of mutual fund managers, there will be winners. Unfortunately—for monkeys, managers *and investors*—the winners are unlikely to repeat.

Bill Miller is a perfect example. Mr. Miller was the manager of Legg Mason Value Trust (LMVTX). His fund is the only mutual fund that was able to beat the S&P 500 Index 15 years in a row. Miller became a celebrity in the mutual fund world, and investors eagerly poured their money into his fund. Unfortunately, like many winning mutual funds, LMVTX plunged to the *bottom 1%* of its Morningstar category over the next 15 years. Remember: Reversion to the Mean, like gravity, does bring us all back to earth.

Many in the financial services industry hate indexing because it is difficult for them to make money selling low-cost index funds. The industry spends billions of dollars attempting to convince us that they can help us beat the market by choosing winning individual stocks, bonds and mutual funds for us. (Fact: They cannot.)

In the 35th anniversary edition of the *Hulbert Financial Digest*, publisher Mark Hulbert wrote that, when he began tracking newsletters in 1980, there were 28 of them. Of those 28, only 9 have survived. The rest are gone. Of the 9 newsletter survivors, only 2 have ever beaten the market (measured by the Wilshire 5000 Total Market Index) on a risk-adjusted basis. Just 2 out of 28; those are pretty poor odds.

The benefits of low-cost index funds and exchange-traded funds (ETFs), which Bogleheads have been preaching about for nearly 20 years, are now becoming more widely known and accepted. The evidence of the superior performance of index funds has become so overwhelming that, in April 2017, the *New York Times* reported that, "thanks to the power of its index funds, Vanguard is pulling in more money than all of the other fund companies in the business."

Bogleheads Speak Out

"The more I struggle to perfect and tilt my portfolio with ever smaller adjustments, the more apparent the inherent wisdom of the 3-fund portfolio becomes. It is a marvelous, straightforward solution to a complex issue. Dare I say, it is a supremely elegant solution."

—TT

"After hours & hours of reading, the light bulb came on. You have probably saved me thousands of dollars & quite literally could make me millions of dollars more."

—SN

"After years of actively 'managing' my own investments, and now nearing retirement, I've decided to take the more passive approach of the three-fund portfolio. After extensive reading on this subject, and from my own personal investing experience, I have become a believer. Its simplicity and long term results are a thing of beauty."

—NY

"Taylor, Thank you for the 3-fund portfolio. At 56 I have been thru 2 advisors, then 5 years of my own efforts chasing alpha, and the light bulb went off last Fall. I moved everything to Vanguard and now I am using the 3-fund portfolio."

—DA

Bernstein's Big-If Paradox

Bill Bernstein, who left his career as a neurologist and became a financial advisor to millionaires, has written a short, 45-page booklet, *If You Can*, intended for millennials but applicable to all investors. He writes,

> Would you believe me if I told you there's an investment strategy that a seven-year-old could understand, that will take you fifteen minutes of work per year, that will outperform 90% of financial professionals in the long run, and that will make you a millionaire over time? Well, it's true. That's it, *if* you can follow this simple recipe throughout your working career, you will almost certainly beat out most professional investors. More importantly, you'll likely accumulate enough savings to retire comfortably.

Bernstein's recipe: Start by saving 15% of your salary at age 25, putting the funds into a 401(k), an IRA, or a taxable account (or all three). Divide your savings into just three different mutual funds:

A U.S. Total Stock Market Index Fund
An International Total Stock Market Index Fund
A U.S. Total Bond Market Index Fund

This great little booklet is currently available as a free PDF at: https://www.etf.com/docs/IfYouCan.pdf.

CHAPTER TWO

John C. Bogle—The Investor's Best Friend[1]

Jack (as he prefers to be called) Bogle is the founder of Vanguard—the only mutual fund company owned by its investors, not by its founder or outside stockholders. This was a tremendous gift to Vanguard investors, since it means that, unlike other fund companies, Vanguard does not use part of investor returns to pay company stockholders. The result is that, after company expenses, all the Vanguard fund returns go to the Vanguard fund investors. The results are remarkable.

---

[1] This book could not have been written without John C. (Jack) Bogle, who invented the first retail index mutual fund and each of the three total market index funds in the Three-Fund Portfolio.

For the 10-year period ending September 30, 2017, 9 of 9 Vanguard money market funds, 55 of 58 Vanguard bond funds, 22 of 22 Vanguard balanced funds, and 128 of 137 Vanguard stock funds—for a total of 214 of 226 Vanguard funds—outperformed their Lipper peer-group average.

—Vanguard Report

Jack Bogle is one of a small handful of people who made the investing world serve the hopes and dreams of ordinary people. Whatever his subject, he speaks and writes from a strong, moral belief that finance should be simple, honest, and fair.

—Jane Bryant Quinn, syndicated columnist and author of *Making the Most of Your Money*

I rank this Bogle invention (index fund) along with the invention of the wheel, the alphabet, the Gutenberg printing press, and wine and cheese: a mutual fund that never made Bogle rich but elevated the long-term returns of the mutual-fund owners.

—Paul Samuelson, Nobel Laureate

The Vanguard advantage is becoming more widely recognized. Vanguard is now the largest mutual fund company in the world, with over $4 trillion in assets. Jack Bogle could easily have become a multi-billionaire by taking a share of his company profits; instead, he chose to give the money back to the investors who own the Vanguard funds.

My wife and I first met Mr. Bogle in February 1999 at *The Money Show* in Orlando, Florida, where Jack was the keynote speaker. Jack describes our first meeting in the Foreword of our first book, *The Bogleheads' Guide to Investing:*

It was not until February 3, 1999, that I met my first Boglehead. The occasion was 'The Money Show' in Orlando, Florida, where I gave a contentious speech about investment principles ("The Clash of the Cultures in Investing: Complexity vs. Simplicity") that at once

watch given to him by a friend while he was in the hospital for his 1996 heart transplant.

k retired as Chairman of Vanguard in 1999. Now, his week-e usually spent in the John C. Bogle Research Center where tinues working on behalf of investors. As you might suspect uch a generous human being, he donates much of his income rity.

k Bogle's contributions to the world have not gone unnoticed. s received hundreds of awards, including being named to *Time* ine's list of "The World's 100 Most Powerful and Influential e" and *Fortune* magazine's "One of the Investment Industry's Giants of the 20th Century."

tatue is ever erected to honor the person who has done the most merican investors, the hands-down choice should be Jack Bogle.

—Warren Buffett, in his 2016 Annual Letter to Berkshire Shareholders

Bogleheads Speak Out

"It is incredible how much knowledge has gone into the simple choices that Taylor proposes."

—UN

"Thanks to the Bogleheads and Taylor Larimore, I have learned that by living below my means and investing in total market index funds using a Three-Fund Portfolio, I will reap my share of the future returns of three broad markets, whatever these returns are."

—LO

"The three-fund portfolio is majestic in its depth of understanding, and simplicity."

—LE

"Thanks for all your generous sharing of time and knowledge to this community and the brilliance of the 3-fund portfolio."

—AL

seemed to confound the hosts who invited
to infuriate the sponsor firms (all offering t
riches), and to amaze and delight the audien
individual investors.

Shortly before my talk, Taylor Larimore
Pat) introduced himself to me. Taylor, then an
unofficial leader of the Bogleheads, proved to b
ing as I've ever met—warm, thoughtful, intellige
and eager to help others. A combat veteran o
an exceptional sailor are only a few aspects of
I mention them because the first demands cou
the second, careful planning and staying the cou
the while adjusting to the winds and tides. These t
are the principal traits of the successful investor.

My next opportunity to meet Mr. Bogle was
Miami in March 2000. He was again the keynote
at the *Miami Herald* "Making Money" seminar.

Mel Lindauer and I had become good friends o
Vanguard Diehards online forum. We extended a
on the forum to anyone who would like to join
the first Boglehead Reunion to be held in my Miam
Inasmuch as Mr. Bogle would be in town for the *Mia
inar, we took a chance that he just might attend our B
We invited him to join us and, as fate would have it,

It was a beautiful evening for the 21 Bogleheads
My late wife, Pat, prepared a delicious Florida lobst
Mr. Bogle told us of the difficulties he experienced wh
to start a new kind of mutual fund company that wo
by its investors. Jack answered all our questions in h
est and forthright way. During the ensuing years, I
privilege of becoming close friends with Jack and his
Eve. Jack was very kind and referred to me as one of his
his 2011 book, *Don't Count On It*. Of course, Jack is the
having the courage to fight the industry in voice, print,
"to give ordinary investors a fair shake."

Today, Mr. Bogle lives with his wife in an unpretenti
near the Vanguard campus. He drives an aging Volvo and

the $14
waiting

Jac
days a
he con
with s
to cha

Ja
He ha
maga
Peopl
Four

If a s
for A

CHAPTER THREE

John Bogle Introduces Three Total Market Index Funds

Now that you know the story of how Jack Bogle and I first met and became such good friends, let's press on to how the rubber meets the road for individual investors like you and me. We will go point by point, benefit by benefit, and make it as easy as one, two, three.

In 1976, Mr. Bogle introduced the world's first retail index mutual fund (the Vanguard 500 Index Fund) containing 500 large U.S. Stocks.

He later determined that a single stock fund containing nearly all U.S. stocks, including large-caps, mid-caps and small-caps, would be an improvement over what was then available.

He also recognized the need for a single, diversified, high-quality bond fund and the demand for international diversification. The result was his introduction of three low-cost, total market index funds:

Vanguard Total Stock Market Index Fund Investor Shares (VTSMX) and Admiral Shares (VTSAX), introduced in 1992, allow investors to own more than 3,500 U.S. company stocks at extremely low cost. Investor Shares ($3,000 minimum) have an expense ratio of 0.15%. Admiral Shares ($10,000 minimum) have an expense ratio of 0.04%. Putting this in dollars means that an investor can invest $10,000 at a cost of only $4 per year. Truly remarkable!

Vanguard Total Bond Market Index Fund Investor Shares (VBMFX) and Admiral Shares (VBTLX), introduced in 1986, allow investors to own more than 8,000 very diversified, high-quality U.S. bonds. The expense ratio (the percentage of a fund's net assets used to pay a portion of its annual expenses) is currently 0.15% for Vanguard's Investor Shares. Admiral Shares have an expense ratio of 0.05%.

Vanguard Total International Stock Index Fund Investor Shares (VGTSX) and Admiral Shares (VTIAX), introduced in 1996, allow investors to hold more than 6,000 international stocks, including emerging market stocks. Investor Shares have an expense ratio of 0.18%. Admiral Shares have an expense ratio of 0.12%.

Thanks to Jack Bogle, for the first time in history ordinary investors can own more than 17,000 diversified, nonoverlapping, worldwide securities at an amazingly low cost.

Investors are catching on. All three of Jack's total market index funds are now the world's largest funds in their category.

I favor the all-market index fund as the best choice for most investors. Don't look for the needle. Buy the haystack.

—Remarks by John Bogle to the Investment Analysts Society

Bogleheads Speak Out

"Taylor's 'Three-Fund Portfolio' postings win hands down for the best thing I've ever read on any finance site, anywhere, ever."

—CL

"As I approach retirement I am more and more aware of the debt I owe to all Bogleheads and specifically to Taylor. His books led me to the 3-Fund Portfolio (+TIPS), which has made all the difference as I approach retirement with a surprising 7-figure portfolio."

—DP

"The simplicity of it, the low expenses, low taxes and diversification is impressive."

—SG

"With all the complicated and confusing messages about investing, the three-fund portfolio is a breath of fresh air and the essence of what John Bogle has taught all these years."

—ST

The Rick Ferri/Alex Benke Study[1]

In June 2013, Rick Ferri, CFA, and his fellow researcher, Alex Benke, CFP, did a 28-page study comparing the returns of the three Vanguard total market index funds in the Three-Fund Portfolio with those of 5,000 portfolios of randomly selected, comparable, actively-managed funds, over 10-year and 16-year periods (2003–2012 and 1997–2012, respectively). Their conclusions, over 16 years, based on learning that the outperformance of the index portfolio was 82.9% were:

- "The longer an index portfolio is held, the better its performance relative to an all actively-managed portfolio."
- "A diversified portfolio holding only index funds in all asset classes is difficult to beat in the short-term and becomes more difficult to beat over time."
- "Investors increase their probability of meeting their investment goals with a diversified all-index fund portfolio held for the long term."

---

[1]Published by Betterment in February 2014.

CHAPTER FOUR

Twenty Benefits of Total Market Index Funds (in no particular order)

BENEFIT 1: NO ADVISOR RISK

The Three-Fund Portfolio is remarkably easy to maintain. For this reason, most three-fund investors can avoid the additional cost and risks of using a broker or a financial advisor.

The search by the elite for superior investment advice has caused it, in aggregate, to waste more than $100 billion over the past decade.

—Warren Buffett in his 2017 Annual Letter to Berkshire Shareholders

---

There are two primary risks when using an advisor: "incompetence" and "conflict of interest."

Incompetence: In most states, the minimum level of education needed to become a broker or a financial advisor is lower than that needed to become a hairdresser or an electrician. Most states do not require even a high school diploma to become a broker or a financial advisor. Financial advisors *are* required to take a state licensing exam that tests basic product knowledge and awareness of the applicable state and federal laws. However, none are required to have any substantive or formal education in financial planning itself.

Conflict of interest: *You* want the lowest cost subtracted from your returns. *Your advisor* wants the largest income for himself and his family. You can guess who is likely to win.

You must understand that whatever the advisor is paid comes out of the return on your investment. The cumulative impact of advisor and broker fees over an investment lifetime can be huge, as the table below shows.

Time Horizon	Annual Fee Rate						
	0.10%	0.25%	0.50%	1.00%	2.00%	3.00%	
3 years	−0.3%	−0.7%	−1.5%	−2.9%	−5.8%	−8.5%	⎫
5 years	−0.5%	−1.2%	−2.5%	−4.9%	−9.4%	−13.7%	⎪
10 years	−1.0%	−2.5%	−4.9%	−9.5%	−18.0%	−25.6%	⎬ Effect on Your
20 years	−2.0%	−4.9%	−9.5%	−18.0%	−32.7%	−44.6%	Investment
30 years	−3.0%	−7.2%	−13.9%	**−25.8%**	−44.8%	−58.8%	⎪
40 years	−3.9%	−9.5%	−18.1%	−32.8%	−54.7%	−69.3%	⎭

Source: Vanguard

Advisor costs *appear* minor and are easily hidden. Several studies have shown that brokers and advisors may actually earn more than their customers. Brokers and advisors can be ethically challenged, and many do not put their clients first. True costs often are hidden in the fine print of statements their clients receive.

Hidden fees are a little bit like high blood pressure. You don't really feel it, and you don't necessarily see it, but it'll eventually kill you.

— Jeff Acheson, CFP

On April 14, 2016, the U.S. Department of Labor proposed a fiduciary rule that would require financial brokers to consider their client's best interest (instead of their own) when offering retirement investing advice. It is not surprising that insurance companies, mutual funds and brokerages, with an army of lobbyists, are vigorously fighting implementation of the fiduciary rule.

Act as if every broker, insurance salesman, mutual fund salesperson and financial advisor you encounter is a hardened criminal, and stick to low-cost index funds, and you'll do just fine.

— William J. Bernstein, author of *If You Can*

I am not saying to avoid all advisors. For those who really need one, a low-cost advisor can be worth the fees charged. A good fiduciary advisor can provide services that many investors may not be able to handle themselves. For example, a good advisor will:

- Help determine your goals and determine how much you'll need to save to reach those goals
- Help structure your most appropriate asset allocation
- Help you stay the course during Bear Markets
- Help with insurance needs (including life, disability, and health care)
- Give advice about taxes, social security, annuities, tax-loss harvesting, rebalancing, order of withdrawals, estate planning, and other financial matters

If you feel you need the services of an advisor, Vanguard offers a Personal Advisory Service. Their non-commissioned, professional advisors currently charge just 0.3% of assets. Services include an in-depth analysis and assistance in transferring assets. You might also check the website of the National Association of Personal Financial Advisors (www.napfa.org) or the Garrett Planning Network (www.garrettplanningnetwork.com). Both organizations list fee-only planners. Using one of these advisors can be much less expensive than paying a percentage of your assets under management (known as AUM) year after year to a commission-based broker or other financial advisor. You should also check with the Securities and Exchange Commission (www.sec.gov/investor/brokers.htm) for any disciplinary history on the registered advisor you are considering using.

The simple, successful Three-Fund Portfolio, which nearly anyone can manage, will significantly reduce your need for an expensive advisor. Investors seeking more advanced information, often in place of an advisor, should read *The Bogleheads' Guide to Investing* and/or *The Bogleheads' Guide to Retirement Planning*.

BENEFIT 2: NO ASSET BLOAT

When a managed fund is flooded with new money, it is very disruptive and usually results in lower returns. This is called "asset bloat." There are several reasons asset bloat is bad:

- As investors rush into a popular active mutual fund, new cash is disruptive because it requires the fund manager to spend more time with additional security analysis. It also increases the fund manager's duties, as it is imperative to get the new cash invested as quickly as possible.
- The manager cannot invest large amounts of cash in a company without impacting the market for that company's stock. This is because a large purchase of company stock will drive up the price of that stock as shares are bought. Market impact is especially true of small-company stocks.
- The fund manager will find it difficult to invest the money in a satisfactory manner because as fund assets rise, the number of appropriate additional stocks shrinks, making it difficult to maintain the fund's objectives. The fund manager also knows that transaction costs, (e.g., commissions, bid-ask spreads, market impact and opportunity costs) will increase, affecting existing fund shareholders.
- Mutual fund regulations prohibit a fund from owning more than 10% of the outstanding voting shares of an issuer. This restriction may prevent a fund manager from buying more shares of company stock that the fund already owns, thereby forcing managers to buy less-desirable securities.

The Fidelity Magellan Fund is often mentioned as a victim of asset bloat. In 1990, the Magellan Fund was the largest mutual fund in the world. Unfortunately for investors who came in late, its returns subsequently plunged to the bottom 1% of its Morningstar category. The result was that many investors in Magellan lost a large part of their life savings.

Vanguard is known for its willingness to close a fund when that fund becomes bloated. In 2016, Vanguard closed its $30.6 billion

Dividend Growth Fund (VDIGX) to new investors. As former Vanguard CEO Bill McNabb explained, "Vanguard is proactively taking steps to slow strong cash flows to help ensure that the advisor's ability to produce competitive long-term results for investors is not compromised."

David Swenson, Yale University Chief Investment Officer and author of *Unconventional Success*, wrote: "Bloated portfolios and excessive fees represent the most visible ways in which mutual fund manager agents extract rents from mutual fund investor principals."

Total Market Index Funds are not affected by asset bloat because all new money is easily distributed among the stocks of thousands of companies.

Bogleheads Speak Out

Dear Taylor: "This 3-fund portfolio and education on index funds has saved me from most of the tensions of investing."

—SA

BENEFIT 3: NO INDEX FRONT RUNNING

"Index front running" is when traders know in advance that an index manager *must sell* a stock because it no longer meets the index specifications. Perhaps a small-cap stock has grown too large for its small-cap index or a value stock has become a growth stock. In both cases, traders know that the index fund manager must sell one or more of its stocks in that category.

This works the same as when a trader knows in advance that an index manager *must buy* a stock to meet the index specifications. Advance knowledge normally lowers the price of a stock to be sold and raises the price of a stock before it is bought, to the detriment of both the index fund manager and the fund investors.

In March 2015, American Airlines announced it would be added to the S&P 500 Index. Between the time of the announcement and the time when the company was added to the index four days later, the company stock increased 11%, thereby increasing the cost to the index and ultimately hurting its performance.

A study by Winton Capital Management Ltd. found that the S&P 500 Index lost 0.2 percentage points from 1990 to 2011 due to front running.

Total Market Index Funds do not suffer the impact of front running because they hold nearly every publicly-listed stock. If a stock is sold by a small-cap index and bought by a mid-cap index, it makes no difference to the passive manager of a total market index fund because the index fund manager neither sells nor buys the stock, thus avoiding front running and other hidden turnover costs.

Bogleheads Speak Out

"I have used the three-fund portfolio for many years with great success."

—DO

BENEFIT 4: NO FUND MANAGER RISK

Since Mr. Bogle's introduction of the first retail index fund, First Index Investment Trust, the financial industry has fought a losing battle, spending billions each year in an attempt to keep investors in expensive and highly profitable (for them) actively managed funds, rather than in low-cost index funds.

A good example of "manager risk" is the Fidelity Magellan Fund (FMAGX), managed by Peter Lynch. Between 1977 and 1990 the fund averaged a 29% annual return, making Magellan the best performing and largest mutual fund in the world.

So, what happened? In 1990 Mr. Lynch decided to retire. A succession of new managers were hired and fired as the Magellan Fund began to underperform the market. Shareholders, many of whom bought near the top, began selling with large losses as the fund's return declined. On January 12, 2018, the Magellan Fund was in the *bottom 11%* of all funds in its Morningstar category for 10-year returns.

Bruce Berkowitz, manager of the Fairholme Fund, is a more recent example of fund manager risk. Berkowitz was Morningstar's "Manager of the Decade" in 2009, but on January 12, 2018, the Fairholme Fund was in the bottom 1% of its category. As of this writing, Mr. Berkowitz remains manager.

Specific Fund Manager Risks

1. **Fund managers** always **leave.** In the case of Peter Lynch, it was because he decided to retire. However, fund managers leave for other reasons: sickness, transfer to another fund, a move to another company. Many fund managers are simply fired for underperformance. Total Market Index funds do not have this problem.

2. **Winning fund managers later underperform.** It seems obvious that a good stock or bond picker should easily outperform an index fund that simply reflects the average stock return. Nevertheless, like Bill Miller and Bruce Berkowitz, whose stories were recounted earlier, most winning fund managers eventually underperform their index benchmark. This is called "Reversion to the Mean."

Warren Buffett has used the "monkey illustration" to explain why it is impossible to know whether a fund manager has outstanding talent or was just lucky: "If 1,000 managers make a market prediction at the beginning of the year, it's very likely that the calls of at least one will be correct for nine consecutive years. Of course, 1,000 monkeys would be just as likely to produce a seemingly all-wise prophet."

Index fund managers make no attempt to pick winning stocks. Their job performance is measured by low cost and by accurately tracking their index.

Of the 355 equity funds in 1970, fully 233 of those funds have gone out of business. Only 24 outpaced the market by more than 1% a year. These are terrible odds.

—Jack Bogle, *The Little Book of Common Sense Investing*

Bogleheads Speak Out

"I find it amazing how quickly a really good idea can gain traction among so many people. Thanks for advocating this remarkable approach to investing. It has done a great deal of good for a large number of people."

—RA

BENEFIT 5: NO INDIVIDUAL STOCK RISK

I remember attending a *Miami Herald* Money Show in March 2000. Unknown at the time, this was the year and month when the U.S. stock market had reached its peak after a long Bull Market and was about to suffer one of the worst Bear Markets since the Great Depression.

Jack Bogle and Jim Cramer (the financial television personality) were the keynote speakers. Jack spoke first and warned the large audience that the stock market was overvalued, and he reminded them about the importance of holding a substantial allocation of high-quality bonds.

When Mr. Bogle finished speaking, it was Mr. Cramer's turn. I was standing in the back of the auditorium with Mel Lindauer, my co-author on two other *Bogleheads'* books. Jim asked the audience to take out a pencil and paper and write down the names of ten individual stocks he would be recommending as sure "winners." Mel and I watched as hundreds of naive investors eagerly wrote down Mr. Cramer's top stock tips. (I couldn't fault them for effort, since I had once tried this on my own.)

Most of the audience seemed sure they were getting important stock tips from a popular media guru, but the way those tips actually played out was a different story. Four years later, in the April 2004 edition of *Barron's* magazine, Alan Abelson wrote, "[Cramer's] 10 dot com bubble picks of 2000 ended up tanking by an average of 90%." Picking individual stocks is very risky, as "Jim Cramer's Top Stock Picks" illustrates.

Unlike mutual funds, individual stocks can plunge to zero. On the 50th birthday of the S&P 500 Index, only 86 of the original 500 companies still remained, showing it is possible to turn a large fortune into a small fortune with individual stocks. On the other hand, it is unheard of for a registered mutual fund to go to zero.

Many investors, especially new ones, attempt to "beat the market" by investing in individual stocks. The temptation is understandable when we read about the fabulous returns (when true) of someone who had the foresight to buy a little-known stock before it became a winner. Stock pickers love to talk about their *good* stock picks, but they seldom, if ever, talk about their *bad* ones.

Daniel Kahneman and Amos Tversky suggested in a 1992 study that people dislike losses twice as much as they like gains.[1] The media (to increase viewing and readership) encourage investors to buy individual stocks by featuring recommendations from "experts," who—more often than not—are proven wrong. We are seldom reminded that many of yesterday's hot stocks (think Kodak, Enron, General Motors and Westinghouse) have turned from winners to losers, leaving most of their investors suffering large losses.

Bogleheads Speak Out

"I've implemented Taylor's three-fund portfolio and stuck with it for years now. My primary reasons are that it is simple, elegant, I understand it, and I sleep well at night."

—FE

---

[1] Econometrica, March 1979.

BENEFIT 6: NO OVERLAP

"Overlap" occurs when two different mutual funds or ETFs share the same securities in a portfolio. So, if an investor owns multiple mutual funds or ETFs that contain the same securities, the result is a less-diversified portfolio.

To minimize risk, investors want funds with securities that act differently. If one stock or bond fund declines in value, we want other stocks or bonds in the portfolio to gain in value. If two funds hold securities that are the same (i.e., overlapped), diversification is reduced and risk increases.

Many company retirement plans do not offer a Total Stock Market Index Fund. Instead, they offer an S&P 500 Index Fund. That's a good substitute, since both funds hold the largest and most successful stocks in the United States, and both have similar long-term risks and returns.

Many times, a company, an educational institution, or a government entity will offer a combination of an S&P 500 Index Fund and an Extended Market Index Fund. Investors can achieve a fund similar to a U.S. Total Market Index Fund by using those two funds, combining 80% S&P 500 Fund with 20% Extended Market Fund. There will be no fund overlap, because Mr. Bogle specifically designed the Extended Market Index Fund to complement the S&P fund by avoiding any individual stock overlap.

The more funds in a portfolio, the greater the chance of fund and securities overlap. You'll be happy to know there is no fund or securities overlap in the Three-Fund Portfolio.

Bogleheads Speak Out

"The 3 fund, total market index portfolio is so easily maintained and sensible that I now have much more time to spend on other pursuits. Things that I once cared about (buying/selling, timing, etc.), quite remarkably, hold little or no interest to me now."

—FA

BENEFIT 7: NO SECTOR RISK

"Market sector risk" is the risk you face when investing in individual sector funds, such as Financials, Healthcare, Real Estate, Energy, Utilities, Gold and Technology, to name a few. The risk is that the sector you choose may perform worse than another sector.

A good example of the risk in sector investing was the popularity of the technology sector in the late 1990s, when technology stocks began to significantly outperform most other sectors. As a result, investors began piling into "hot" technology funds. Unfortunately for them, the tech-heavy NASDAQ Index lost 77.9% during the 2000–2002 Bear Market, thereby wiping out a lifetime of savings for many investors.

Another example of sector risk is Vanguard's Mining and Precious Metals Fund, originally named "Vanguard Gold Fund," which has been Vanguard's most volatile fund. In 1993, Vanguard Gold Fund gained +93.4%—the best return of any Vanguard fund. Fund assets exploded as investors scrambled to buy shares. Unfortunately for those investors, Vanguard Gold Fund began its "reversion to the mean", which is what usually happens to top performing funds. By December 2000, Vanguard Gold Fund had the worst 5- and 10-year returns of all Vanguard funds.

There is no reason (except speculation and industry marketing) to add risky sector funds to a portfolio. Vanguard's two Total Market Equity Funds *already* contain the market weight of sector funds— and with much less risk, cost and complexity.

Bogleheads Speak Out

"Tired of experimenting, sticking with this 3 fund: 70% Stock, 15% Bond, 15% Int'l Stock."

—FI

BENEFIT 8: NO STYLE DRIFT

"Style drift" is the divergence of a mutual fund or an ETF from its stated investment style (focus). Most investors want a combination of at least several styles for their diversification benefit—meaning that when one style is doing badly another style may be doing well.

Stock funds: Morningstar divides stock funds into nine style categories, ranging from large-cap value (considered less risky) to small-cap growth (considered more risky). It is difficult for the manager of a fund to maintain the fund's style because small stocks get larger and mid-cap stocks can get smaller or larger. Value funds can become blend funds or even growth funds. Style risk may also cause a tax problem in taxable accounts, where exchanging a profitable fund because of its style change may result in a capital gains tax.

Bond funds: Morningstar also divides bond funds into nine style categories ranging from short-term high-quality bonds (least risky to long-term low-quality bonds (most risky). Bond funds have a similar style-drift problem. As a bond fund's portfolio ages, long-term bonds become mid-term, mid-term bonds become short-term, and short-term bonds reach maturity. This is a prime reason for the high turnover in most bond funds.

The bottom line: Total market index funds include *all* investment styles within their three broad categories (U.S. stocks, U.S. bonds, and International stocks). For this reason, the total market index funds in The Three-Fund Portfolio do not have a style drift problem. For you and me, that's one less variable to worry about.

Bogleheads Speak Out

"The simplicity as I get older and worry about how others may have to step in someday to help manage things is a huge advantage to me of this portfolio."

—FK

BENEFIT 9: LOW TRACKING ERROR

"Tracking error" is the difference between a fund's return and the return of its chosen index benchmark. A primary goal of index fund managers is to track their benchmark index as closely as possible. Vanguard recently reported that Total Stock Market has lagged its index an average of only 0.14% since its inception, Total International lagged by 0.29% and Total Bond Market by 0.29%. Compared to managed funds, these are very low tracking rates and were the result of good management, great diversification, low volatility, and low cost.

Tracking error may not be noticeable when it's small. However, when tracking error is negative over long periods, or significant over short periods (both of which happen to *actively*-managed and sector funds), the fund's investors may be tempted to change to a better-performing "hot" fund—one of the worst mistakes investors can make.

Bogleheads Speak Out

"I think it's difficult to go wrong with the three-fund solution. I've also learned that it can make one's life much simpler when it comes to rebalancing, portfolio tracking and taxes. Thank you Taylor for nudging me in this direction a few years ago."

—FR

BENEFIT 10: ABOVE-AVERAGE RETURN

A total market fund will never beat the market. But you are guaranteed to do far better than most active investors.

—Jonathan Clements, author of six financial books and more than a thousand columns for the *Wall Street Journal*

Would *you* like to own a three-fund portfolio that is mathematically certain to outperform most amateur and professional investors? Well, you can. Each fund in *The Bogleheads' Guide to the Three-Fund Portfolio* is guaranteed to do just that. Skeptical? You should be. (It's a sign of a good investor).

There are many academic studies showing that index funds nearly always beat their managed funds counterparts. Here are a few:

S&P Dow Jones SPIVA Scorecard: In 2002, S&P Dow Jones Indices introduced its first SPIVA Scorecard, which is the most reliable data comparing managed funds with index funds. Below are quotes from the 2017 year-end SPIVA report:

"Over the 15-year period ending December 2017, 83.7% of large-cap, 95.4% of mid-cap, and 93.21% of small-cap managers trailed their respective (index) benchmarks."

"Across all time horizons, the majority of managers across all international equity categories underperformed their benchmarks."

"Funds disappear at a significant rate. Over the 15-year period, more than 58% of domestic equity funds were either merged or liquidated. Similarly, almost 52% of global/international equity funds and 49% of fixed-income funds were merged or liquidated. This finding highlights the importance of addressing survivorship bias in mutual fund analysis." (Funds with poor results are the ones normally merged or liquidated.)

National Association of College and University Business Officers (NACUBO): Colleges can afford to buy the investment advice of the best and most expensive portfolio managers to handle their endowments, so it is interesting to see their results: According to a press release issued in January 2017, data collected for NACUBO show that "reporting institutions' endowments returned an average of -1.9% (net of fees) for the 2016 fiscal year (July 1, 2015–June 30, 2016)" and "contributed to a decline in long-term 10-year average annual returns to 5.0%—well below the median 7.4% that most institutions report they need to earn in order to maintain their endowments' purchasing power after spending, inflation, and investment management costs." (Meanwhile, the Russell 3,000 Total Market Index returned 7.4%.)

Allan Roth study: Mr. Roth, is a CPA, CFP, and fee-only financial advisor. He writes the monthly *Investing* column for AARP magazine and is the author of *How a Second Grader Beats Wall Street* (using The Three-Fund Portfolio).

For this wonderful book, written in 2009, Allan did a study to determine the probability that an all-active fund portfolio will beat an all-index fund portfolio—when the index fund expense ratio was 0.23 and the managed fund ratio was 2.0. The table prepared by Allan shows that one managed fund had a 42% chance of beating an all-index fund over a 1-year period, but that the chances become less and less as more funds are added and as the length of time increases, until there is only a 1% chance with ten active funds after 25 years.

	1 Year	5 Years	10 Years	25 Years
One Active Fund	42%	30%	23%	12%
Five Active Funds	32%	18%	11%	3%
Ten Active Funds	25%	9%	6%	1%

Rick Ferri study: Mr. Ferri, CFA, is a retired financial advisor and the author of six highly regarded financial books. As described in Chapter 3, Mr. Ferri did a study of 5,000 randomly selected portfolios of actively-managed mutual funds and compared them to the funds in The Three-Fund Portfolio. The study's conclusion: "Dedicated active-fund investors can look forward to a 99% probability their portfolio will underperform an all-index fund portfolio over their lifetime."

William Sharpe paper: William Sharpe, Nobel Laureate, wrote "The Arithmetic of Active Management" for the *Financial Analysts Journal* in 1991 and came to the following conclusion (italic mine): "Properly measured, the average actively-managed dollar *must* underperform the average passively-managed dollar, net of costs. Empirical analyses that appear to refute this principle are guilty of improper measurement."

Paul Samuelson, Nobel Laureate: "Statistically, a broad-based stock index fund will outperform most actively-managed equity portfolios" (from "Challenge to Judgment," the lead article in the 1974 inaugural edition of the *Journal of Portfolio Management*).

On January 12, 2018, Paul Farrell's "Lazy Portfolios" column reported total returns for eight professionally-designed Lazy Portfolios for one, three, five, and ten-year periods. The Second Grader's Starter Portfolio, consisting of The Three-Fund Portfolio of total market index funds, topped all the others—another real-world report showing that The Three-Fund Portfolio, as espoused in this book, works over multiple time periods.

The financial industry does not want us to know that index funds have higher returns than managed funds because they make their money promoting higher-cost managed funds. In an attempt to disparage index funds, one large broker-dealer, Sanford C. Bernstein & Co. LLC, described passive investing as promoting a system of capital allocation worse than Marxism. Nevertheless, the tide is turning. At the end of 2016, index funds (including ETFs) represented 24.9% of all equity funds, and the percentage is rapidly increasing as investors learn about indexing's higher returns.

As an investor, you have a choice: You can be like the gamblers who try to beat the casino, or you can *be* the casino by investing in total market index funds. It's an easy choice, once you understand the odds.

Bogleheads Speak Out

"Investing can be simple when you just trust a few broad stock and bond indices, choose an appropriate asset allocation, and stick to your plan."

—FO

You Can't Beat the Market

Jonathan Clements is one of the most knowledgeable financial writers in the business. He spent almost 20 years at The *Wall Street Journal*, where he wrote over a thousand columns on personal finance, before leaving to become director of Financial Education at Citigroup. Mr. Clements is the author of six highly-regarded books on finance and now writes a personal finance newsletter, *The Humble Dollar.* Here is the first sentence in the March 2018 edition of that newsletter: "TRYING TO BEAT THE MARKET isn't just a risky endeavor that will almost certainly end in failure. It's also unnecessary and, arguably, an astonishing waste of money and time."

BENEFIT 11: SIMPLIFIED CONTRIBUTIONS AND WITHDRAWALS

One problem for investors holding multi-fund portfolios is that each contribution and each withdrawal must be spread among all the funds in the portfolio in order to maintain the desired portfolio asset allocation. Having only two stock funds and one bond fund makes this task considerably easier and more efficient.

Let's take a look at how that works for an investor with a portfolio of a larger number of mutual funds. Many of these types of portfolios contain at least some active funds and often include some balanced funds. In this case, there could well be overlap among the funds, since the balanced funds contain some equities and some bonds. As a result, investors making contributions or withdrawals would need to closely examine the current breakdown in each of their funds to determine their current asset allocation, prior to making any contributions or withdrawals. Since there is no overlap between equities and bonds in The Three-Fund Portfolio, this makes contributions and withdrawals far simpler.

Bogleheads Speak Out

"Simply owning a broad market index fund greatly simplifies the strategy for accumulating and coming up with a withdrawal strategy."

—JO

BENEFIT 12: THE BENEFIT OF CONSISTENCY

Investors appreciate a mutual fund or an ETF that is consistent, compared with a fund that is volatile, changes managers, changes style or takes unnecessary risk in the hope of market-beating performance.

Vanguard Total Stock Market Index Fund is known for its consistency when compared to other stock funds. As of this writing, Vanguard Total Stock Market Index Fund Admiral Shares (VTSAX) has beaten its Morningstar category average every year since its inception in 2001. Very few funds can claim this consistency. One of the greatest benefits of total market index funds is that you will never have to worry about your portfolio underperforming the market, because you own the market.

In 2007, the Vanguard Energy Fund Admiral Shares (VGELX) had a very good year. It gained 34.81% compared to the Vanguard Total Stock Market Index Fund, which gained 5.57%. Investors rushed into energy funds to enjoy anticipated profits, but the table following shows what happened during the next 10 years.

VTSAX vs VGELX, COMPARATIVE ANNUAL RETURNS

Year	VTSAX	VGELX
2008	-36.99	-39.34
2009	28.83	24.85
2010	17.36	21.10
2011	1.08	2.79
2012	16.38	3.49
2013	33.52	25.78
2014	12.56	9.88
2015	0.39	-28.22
2016	12.66	28.94
2017	21.17	-2.39
10-Year Avg	9.71	1.89

Bogleheads Speak Out

"This three-fund portfolio is what my wife and I now use for our retirement savings."

—MP

BENEFIT 13: LOW TURNOVER

"Turnover" is the ratio of how much of a fund's securities are replaced each year. For example, if a mutual fund invests in 100 different stocks and 50 of them are replaced during one year, the turnover ratio would be 50%. All mutual funds and ETFs have turnover.

Following are recent turnover rates for each Vanguard fund in The Three-Fund Portfolio compared with the turnover rates of all funds in the same category:

Fund	Turnover	Category Average
Total Stock Market	4%	59%
Total International	3%	60%
Total Bond Market	61%	232%

Source: Morningstar

Mr. Bogle suggests, as a rule of thumb, that turnover costs are equal to about one percent of a fund's assets. Turnover costs (which are hidden from investors) include commissions, spreads, impact and administrative costs. Turnover costs do not include the additional tax cost to investors when the turnover results in capital gains distributions to the investor. Turnover costs often are larger than a fund's published expense ratio (i.e., management fees and operating expenses combined).

Morningstar reported that for the 10 years ending in December 2016, the average U.S. diversified equity fund returned 5.15%. However, primarily because of higher turnover and bad market timing, fund investors averaged only a 4.30% annual return. That difference hurts all of us, so we should do everything we can to minimize it.

Total market index funds have among the lowest stock and bond turnover rates. The result is extremely low turnover costs for Three-Fund Portfolio investors, with the savings meaning higher returns for all of us.

Bogleheads Speak Out

"Finally, after years of tinkering, I have the true Three-Fund portfolio you inspired."

—RW

BENEFIT 14: LOW COSTS

Most of us have learned from experience that cheap goods and services are usually not as good as more expensive goods and services. Paying more will often buy a better house, a better car, better clothing, better airline seats, and better service. It is, therefore, understandable that many investors believe that paying more for expensive funds, expensive financial advice, and expensive investments will result in better results.

The opposite is nearly always true. Investing in a simple three-fund portfolio of total market index funds eliminates the need to choose from among pricey funds, advisors and individual investments, thus putting more money in your pocket and less in theirs.

Fund costs are key to your ultimate returns.

In our *Bogleheads' Guide to Investing*, we reported on a study done by Financial Research Corporation to determine which mutual fund predictors really worked:

* Morningstar STAR ratings
* Past performance
* Turnover
* Expenses
* Manager tenure
* Net sales
* Asset size
* Alpha (excess return)
* Beta (volatility)
* Standard deviation
* Sharpe Ratio

This was their conclusion: "**The expense ratio is the only reliable predictor of future mutual fund performance.**"

Morningstar (a primary source for reliable mutual fund data) did a similar study and came to the same conclusion: "If there's anything in the whole world of mutual funds that you can take to the bank, it's that expense ratios help you make a better decision. In every single time period and data point tested, low-cost funds beat high-cost funds."

In 2014 Mr. Bogle did a study of total fund costs (before taxes) for the CFA Institute. Here are his findings:

ALL-IN INVESTMENT EXPENSES FOR RETIREMENT PLAN INVESTORS

	Actively-Managed Funds	Index Funds
Expense Ratio	1.12%	0.06%
Transaction Costs	0.50%	0.00%
Cash Drag	0.15%	0.00%
Sales Charges/Fees	0.50%	0.00%
All-in Expenses	2.27%	0.06%

Mr. Bogle understates the index fund advantage, because tax costs were not included. He once estimated that "taxes have in the past cost fund investors an extra 1.5% percent per year compared to holding the market portfolio."

Total market index funds have costs, but they are much lower than managed-fund costs. One reason is that total market funds have extremely low turnover. Unlike most mutual funds and ETFs, total market index funds do not need to buy or sell stocks when a company moves from one category to another. Turnover often results in a capital gain in other funds, which is then passed on to the fund's owners.

The three mutual funds in The Three-Fund Portfolio enjoy extremely low costs:

FUND	EXPENSE RATIO	2016 INDUSTRY AVERAGE
Total Stock Market Investor Shares (VTSMX)	0.15%	0.48%
Total Stock Market Admiral Shares (VTSAX)	0.04%	0.48%
Total Stock Market ETF Shares (VTI)	0.04%	NA
Total International Investor Shares (VGTSX)	0.18%	0.70%
Total International Admiral Shares (VTIAX)	0.11%	0.70%
Total International ETF (VXUS)	0.11%	NA
Total Bond Market Investor Shares (VBMFX)	0.15%	0.48%
Total Bond Market Admiral Shares (VBTLX)	0.05%	NA
Total Bond Market ETF (BND)		

Minimum investment: Investor Shares $3,000, Admiral Shares $10,000
Source: Vanguard and Morningstar (2017)

To give you an idea of the impact of costs, consider this: If stocks gain an average of 6% annually during the next 30 years, someone who invested $25,000 with a 1% yearly fee will forego more than $35,500 in gains because of the fee— *more than the original investment!*

Like Mr. Bogle, I believe that the hard-earned money saved and invested should be yours.

You get to keep exactly what you don't pay for.

—Jack Bogle, *The Little Book of Common Sense Investing*

Bogleheads Speak Out

"The simplicity of it, the low expenses, low taxes and diversification is impressive."

—SG

BENEFIT 15: MAXIMUM DIVERSIFICATION (LOWER RISK)

If there is one thing about investing on which all authorities agree, it is the benefit of diversification, often called "the only free lunch in investing."

The primary benefit of diversification is that diversified mutual fund investors will never have all their investments in an underperforming fund, thus having a much greater chance of achieving their goals.

The Three-Fund Portfolio contains more than 15,000 worldwide securities for the ultimate diversification. Wall Street may try to sell you a more complex (and expensive) portfolio, but it is unlikely to be more diversified. The world, in a sense, becomes your oyster.

According to Morningstar, the level of risk contained in the stocks that are represented in the S&P 500 and the Wilshire 5000 total market index is about 25% less than the risk in the average active stock fund.

The Lehman Brothers bankruptcy in 2008 is an example of the need for diversification. Lehman Brothers was founded in 1850, and in 2000 it was the fourth largest investment bank in the United States. In the 2008 Bear Market, Lehman Brothers went bankrupt, causing thousands of their employees and individual investors who owned Lehman Brothers shares to lose all, or part, of their retirement benefits and life savings.

Vanguard Total Stock Market Index Fund investors also owned Lehman Brothers shares in their fund, but because their fund was diversified with thousands of other stocks, Total Stock Market fund shareholders were little affected by the bankruptcy. This is another advantage for total market index funds: Because all your stocks and bonds are wrapped into one fund, you don't see the carnage that unnerves other investors, causing them to worry and sell at exactly the wrong time (i.e., during Bear Markets).

Diversification, with its lower risk, is the hallmark of The Three-Fund Portfolio. It protects us from allowing our brain—wired to sometimes flee out of fear—to become our own worst enemy.

Bogleheads Speak Out

"I am a three-fund portfolio guy and we all agree with John Bogle in that simplicity in investing is a great option."

—RB

BENEFIT 16: PORTFOLIO EFFICIENCY
(BEST RISK/RETURN RATIO)

Total market index funds are highly efficient, due to the fact that they offer the highest return for the amount of risk. This extremely important benefit is little known by the majority of investors and it gets little notice in the press.

"Portfolio efficiency" gets into higher mathematics, so I will let John Norstad, a retired mathematician at Northwestern University, explain:

"Many people do not understand why the cap-weighted total US stock market (TSM) plays such a central role in financial economics. They believe that TSM is just one of many possible US stock portfolios, with no good reason to believe that it is special or superior to other kinds of stock portfolios. They often present alternatives which they claim offer a higher expected return than TSM with less risk. In technical terms, these alternatives are 'more efficient' than TSM. We give three proofs that, under three different assumptions, TSM is efficient in the sense that *no other U.S. stock portfolio can be more efficient than TSM (have lower risk and higher expected return).*" (Italics mine.)

No one can predict the future, but it is reassuring for The Three-Fund Portfolio investors to know they hold a very "efficient" portfolio.

Bogleheads Speak Out

"I'm a fan of Taylor's 3-fund portfolio, Total Stock, Total international Stock and Total Bond Index Funds. That is all you really need and it is pretty simple. Balance once a year to maintain your AA and you are done."

—SI

BENEFIT 17: LOW MAINTENANCE

All portfolios, like a good car that keeps on running, require regular maintenance:

- Funds need rebalancing.
- Contributions and withdrawals change.
- New fund offerings need consideration.
- Funds are merged and liquidated.
- Asset-allocation may need adjustment.
- Changes in income, expenses and net-worth may require adjustment.
- Changes in tax laws and the investor's tax bracket may require adjustments.
- Beneficiaries change.

These and other maintenance items require knowledge, time and attention.

The need for portfolio maintenance, and the opportunity for mistakes, is magnified in direct proportion to the number of funds in a portfolio.

The Three-Fund Portfolio, with only three total market index funds, requires minimum maintenance. This means investors will have less worry and thus may spend more time with family and friends, doing whatever they enjoy. I promise you will learn to appreciate all the repairs or fixes that are *not* required with operating such a simple portfolio.

Bogleheads Speak Out

"The Three-Fund Portfolio has served my family well, and I hope it'll be for many decades to come."

—TY

BENEFIT 18: EASY TO REBALANCE

"Rebalancing" takes place when it's necessary for an investor to exchange fund shares in a portfolio to maintain the portfolio's desired asset allocation.

Knowledgeable investors understand that, more than anything else, the stock/bond ratio in a portfolio determines our *expected* return and *expected* risk. For this reason, it's very important to maintain one's desired asset allocation between stocks and bonds. (We'll talk more about asset allocation in Chapter 5).

The values of the securities in stock and bond funds change constantly. Small changes don't matter, but over time the value of individual funds, especially stock funds, can change substantially. This requires rebalancing, which, in taxable accounts, can trigger capital gains taxes.

In another form of rebalancing, each of the funds in The Three-Fund Portfolio *automatically* adjusts its holdings to match its index benchmark on an almost-daily basis. Although it requires buying and selling securities by the fund managers, this *internal* rebalancing within each fund only rarely results in capital gains distributions to total market shareholders.

While it is necessary for investors to rebalance the three total market index fund portfolio to maintain the desired asset-allocation, this rebalancing is easier and more often results in a much smaller capital gains tax.

Bogleheads Speak Out

"3-fund portfolio, I'm a big fan, keep it simple!"

—OH

BENEFIT 19: TAX EFFICIENCY

Smart investors want to keep their taxes as low as possible. Index funds, especially total market index funds, are among the most tax efficient of all funds when located in taxable accounts. (Tax efficiency isn't a factor in tax-advantaged accounts such as IRAs, 401Ks, 403Bs, etc.)

The tax cost ratio measures how much a fund's annualized return is reduced by the taxes investors have to pay on distributions. (For example, if a fund had a 2% tax cost ratio, it means that investors in that fund lost 2% of their assets to taxes.) According to Morningstar (January 12, 2018), the average tax cost ratio for equity funds tends to fall between 1 and 1.2%. As of this writing, Vanguard Total Stock Market Index Fund has a 15-year tax cost ratio of 0.40—less than half the tax cost ratio of the average equity fund.

The tax efficiency of total stock market index funds derives from several sources:

- **Lower turnover by the passive fund manager**, who doesn't need to exchange stocks that trigger taxes that are later passed on to fund shareholders as distributions. Unlike most equity funds, Vanguard Total Stock Market Index Fund and Total International Stock Index Fund haven't distributed a taxable capital gain since 2000.
- **Lower turnover by the individual investor**, because there is no need to buy and sell total market stock funds, triggering personal taxes. (Total Stock Market Index Fund *already* owns nearly every listed stock.) Likewise, there should be no need to sell Total Bond Market Index Fund shares, since it automatically maintains its broad diversification.
- **Eligibility for lower tax rate**. Vanguard Total Stock Market and Total International Index Funds are eligible for a reduced federal tax rate called "Qualified Dividend Income" (QDI). In 2017 Total U.S. Stock Market had 92% of its distributions qualify for the lower QDI rate while Total International Stock Fund and its ETF had 71% of its distributions eligible for the lower QDI rate. (Bonds are not eligible for the QDI rate, which is one reason taxable bond funds are usually best placed in tax-advantaged accounts.)

Investors should never forget that it's the after-tax returns that count.

Bogleheads Speak Out

"I'm going to once again vouch for the three-fund portfolio and thank Taylor for helping us years ago. What we have been saving in tax and expense ratio probably pays more than half our total living expenses for the year alone."

—HU

BENEFIT 20: SIMPLICITY (FOR INVESTORS, CAREGIVERS, AND HEIRS)

Jack Bogle likes to say, "Simplicity is the master key to financial success." His words ring loud and clear, in contrast to the financial industry that tries to convince us that investing is so complicated we must buy their expensive products and services if we want to be successful investors. **Nothing could be further from the truth.**

Bill Schultheis, advisor and author of *The Coffeehouse Investor*, also wrote about simplicity: "When you simplify your investment decisions, not only do you enrich your life by spending more time with families, friends and careers, you enhance portfolio returns in the process."

According to The Investment Company Institute, in 2016 there were 8,066 mutual funds from which investors were able to choose. Fund marketing can be subtle, but most mutual fund companies try to convince investors that their funds will do (or have done) better than other companies' funds. (Vanguard does not compare company returns.)

One of the most frequent requests on the Bogleheads' online forum is for help with simplifying a portfolio. For example, we recently had a request to help a new Boglehead "track" his portfolio, which contained a mish-mash of 90 overlapping securities. The forum participant didn't realize that "tracking" wasn't his problem. His primary problem was his very confusing and complex high-cost portfolio—the result of using several advisors who were friends and relatives.

This confused investor didn't realize that a simple three-fund portfolio contains more stocks and more bonds (and at a much lower cost) than his unwieldy portfolio of 90 individual securities.

A portfolio with fewer (and larger) funds has many advantages:

- Lower costs
- Fewer hidden turnover costs
- Better tax efficiency
- Avoidance of low-balance fees

- Less distortion from contributions and withdrawals
- Less rebalancing
- Lesser chance of errors
- Easier tax preparation
- Less paperwork, storage
- Less stress
- More free time with family and friends

Simple to understand and maintain, the Three-Fund Portfolio does not require higher mathematics, spreadsheets, complicated tax returns, being glued to the television before, during, and after market hours, or reading the *Wall Street Journal*.

My personal portfolio, all with Vanguard, requires very little maintenance. I use the Vanguard website a few times a year to check for fraud or mistakes. (It has never happened). I am over 70 ½ years old, so I use their website once a year to take the Required Minimum Distributions from my retirement plan. (Vanguard mails me a statement every year showing how much I must withdraw. Thank you, Vanguard.) My year-end Vanguard statement gives me the balance of each of my three funds and is all I need to rebalance to my desired asset allocation. I probably spend about an hour a year managing my stay-the-course portfolio. I leave it to you to imagine what you can do with all the time you will be saving investing in this way.

My simple portfolio is not just very easy for me to manage; it will be easy for my ultimate caregivers and my heirs to manage.

There seems to be some perverse human characteristic that likes to make easy things difficult.

—Warren Buffett

Many Bogleheads add a signature line at the bottom of their forum posts—something that expresses an idea we want to share. I chose this quote from Jack Bogle, as I find it one of his most important messages: **"Simplicity is the master key to financial success."**

Bogleheads Speak Out

"I am convinced that the three-fund portfolio makes the most sense for me as someone who likes to sleep."

—KO

Be Like Mike

Financial Ramblings is a wonderful blog, written by Mike— middle-aged, married, four kids in school. Don't know his last name, but it's unimportant to my story. Perhaps Mike's like you. He's worked hard, made (mostly) good decisions, and with his wife's help, put his family in good financial shape. Mortgage paid. No consumer debt. A sizeable and growing investment portfolio, created while raising a family. No silver spoon, humble beginnings for Mike. To make it all happen, Mike says he answered two questions, and made allocations to three funds. This did wonders for the family's financial health.

Question 1: What is your preference on stock vs. bond allocation? He asks you to remember one important fact: Increasing your equity allocation increases your expected returns, but there also will be greater risks. Your bond allocation is a buffer, as it should represent what you cannot afford to lose. He notes, however, that adding a small amount of stocks to an all-bond portfolio actually increases return while reducing risk. Diversification wins.

Question 2: Domestic vs. international stock mix? Once you've decided on an appropriate stock/bond allocation, you need to decide on your preferred mix of domestic vs. international equities. Why should you bother with international equities? For the diversification benefit. Historical data on international equities shows that this diversification offers you the potential to increase returns while simultaneously reducing volatility. As with the addition of stocks to an all-bond portfolio, this is a classic win-win.

It's also worth keeping in mind that the U.S. stock market accounts for just about one-third of the world's total market capitalization. That being said, you probably don't want to go overboard with the international equities.

Mike suggests the end result might be a standard 60/40 stock/bond mix, with 20% investment in international stocks.

To jumpstart the process, Mike shares the ticker symbols for appropriate index funds from several major fund families:

Vanguard: VTSMX, VGTSX, VBMFX
Fidelity: FSTMX, FSGDX, FBIDX
Schwab: SWTSX, SWISX, SWLBX
TIAA-CREF: TINRX, TRIEX, TBILX

Mike has other alternatives. You can use ETFs (e.g., VTI, VXUS, and BND, or the equivalents from other fund families) if that's what you'd prefer. And if you're in the government's Thrift Savings Plan, you can assemble a portfolio similar to the above, using the C Fund, I Fund, and F (or G) Fund.

One tip to remember: From there, you can reduce your need to rebalance by directing new money (and/or dividend reinvestments) into whichever asset class is low versus the target. This will keep your allocations in your comfort zone, only requiring minimal rebalancing when percentage allocations drift too far from your targets.

Source: "Investing with a Three Fund Portfolio," *Financial Ramblings*, May 13, 2013,   http://www.financialramblings.com/archives/investing-with-a-three-fund-portfolio/

CHAPTER FIVE

Getting Started

For many years after Jack Bogle introduced his three total market index funds, Vanguard was the only mutual fund company where total market index funds were available. However, as word spread, Schwab, Fidelity, and a few other companies each introduced total market index funds with similar low costs. Investors are now able to construct The Three-Fund Portfolio with whichever company they prefer.

Your first step when getting started is to decide which funds best suit your needs and wants. I hope you are convinced that three low-cost total market index funds are ideal and usually all you need. It is permissible to add more funds, but recognize that adding funds to your Three-Fund Portfolio will add cost and complexity.

Your second step in designing your Three-Fund Portfolio is to decide your most suitable asset allocation. *This is your most important investment decision* because, with the exception of the amount you are saving and investing, your asset allocation (i.e., your stock/bond ratio) determines your *expected* return and *expected* risk. (Remember that expected risk and expected return go hand in hand: The higher the expected return, the higher the expected risk. The Vanguard table shows the average annual return and the worst single-year return of various stock and bond allocations from 1926 to 2015:

Stock/Bond Percentage	Average Annual Return	Worst Single-Year Return
0% Stocks / 100% Bonds	5.4%	-8.1%
20% Stocks / 80% Bonds	6.7%	-10.1%
40% Stocks / 60% Bonds	7.8%	-18.4%
60% Stocks / 40% Bonds	8.7%	-26.6%
80% Stocks / 20% Bonds	9.5%	-34.9%
100% Stocks / 0% Bonds	10.1%	-43.1%

The table clearly shows the importance of our overall stock/bond ratio. A high percentage of stocks in a portfolio is more volatile and thus likely to result in both higher returns and greater losses.

Statistics often conceal more than they reveal. For example, what is not shown in the table is the fact that Bear Markets usually last much longer than one year. Therefore, stocks and bonds may have much worse returns than shown for a single year. For example, in the 2008 Bear Market Vanguard Total Stock Market (VTSMX) declined for 16 long months for a total decline of 50.9%. The fund then took another 37 months to recover to its former value. In the same Bear Market, Vanguard Total International Fund (VGTSX) plunged 58.5%. Meanwhile, Vanguard Total Bond Market (VBMFX) *gained* + 5% in 2008.

Vanguard has a free Asset Allocation Tool that you can use to help you decide your most appropriate asset allocation between stocks and bonds. This is the link:

https://personal.vanguard.com/us/FundsInvQuestionnaire?
cbdInitTransUrl=https%3A//personal.vanguard.com/us/funds/tools

Vanguard also has a relationship with Financial Engines, a company that Nobel Laureate Bill Sharpe founded, and it can create awareness about the inherent risks in your portfolio through the use of Monte Carlo simulations. While the future is uncertain, these simulations can share with you the probabilities of future outcomes so you may make informed decisions about the investment risk you are taking as you travel through time.

The basic rule of thumb is to keep your "safe money" (i.e., money you don't want to risk in stocks) in high-quality bonds. While this doesn't give you 100% protection against losses at all times, as you can see in the table above, it has still proven to be valuable advice over time.

Your age in bonds is a good starting point. Using that general rule, a 30-year-old might have 30% in bonds. However, if you want to be more aggressive, you'd have less than your age in bonds; and if you want to be more conservative, you might consider having more than your age in bonds.

The table and the Vanguard Asset Allocation Tool ignore the percentage of your stock allocation that should be invested in international stocks. This is one of the most controversial subjects in investing because of concerns about poor accounting controls and government problems in some foreign countries, lack of transparency, currency exchange risk issues, and other concerns associated with foreign investing. Jack Bogle says he's fine with 0% international but feels that 20% may be okay for investors who want some international exposure.

No one can forecast the stock and bond markets; nevertheless, we *must* make a decision. I suggest that for U.S. investors, 20% of your equity (stocks) should be placed in a total international stock index fund like the Vanguard Total International Stock Market Index Fund (VTIAX). My suggested 20% is a compromise between the *maximum* 20% suggested by Jack Bogle and the *minimum* 20% recommended by a Vanguard study.

Your third step, after determining your desired asset allocation, is to decide whether to use traditional mutual funds or exchange-traded funds (ETFs). This should not be a difficult decision because it doesn't make much difference unless you are a trader. (ETFs are traded on the open market.) Traders prefer ETFs because they may easily be traded nearly any time of day. Bogleheads shun day trading. We are stay-the-course investors.

Vanguard ETFs are simply another share class of their mutual funds. They hold the same securities as their corresponding mutual funds and are equally tax efficient. They also have the same expense ratios as Vanguard Admiral shares. I suggest you start your portfolio with Vanguard mutual funds, and if you later change your mind, you may switch to the fund's corresponding ETFs without tax consequences or other costs. However, the reverse is not allowed (i.e., you cannot switch from Vanguard ETFs to Vanguard mutual funds without selling). Different mutual fund companies will, of course, have different rules.

Your fourth step (if you qualify) is to invest in a tax-advantaged retirement plan.

If you participate in a company retirement plan, you are allowed to make tax-advantaged contributions up to $18,000 annually ($24,000 if age 50 or older). Look first to see if your company plan has a low-cost Target Retirement Fund with a stock/bond mix close to your desired asset allocation. A Target Retirement Fund is an all-in-one fund that automatically adjusts the mix of stocks, bonds and cash according to a selected time frame. These funds automatically rebalance and get more conservative as you age. If you later find that you need to make a change in your fund selection for any reason, there is no tax or penalty for switching to a different fund within most retirement accounts.

It's important to note that not all Target Retirement Funds with the same year in their name contain the same allocation between stocks and bonds, so it's important that you "look under the hood" and select the fund that most closely matches your desired asset allocation. When choosing your fund, remember that it's your desired asset allocation that should be the determining factor, not the date in the fund name.

Retirement funds are designed by company experts. It's hard to go wrong when putting a low-cost target date fund that's suitable for your time frame, risk tolerance, and personal financial situation into your tax-advantaged account

If there are no low-cost target funds available in your company plan, look for low-cost index funds. Most company plans offer an S&P 500 Index Fund, which is a suitable replacement for the U.S. Total Market Index Fund. Some company plans offering an S&P 500 Index fund will also offer an Extended Market Index fund. These two funds together, in a ratio of 5:1 (five of the 500 Index to one of the Extended Market), are about the same as a single U.S. Total Market Index Fund.

If your company plan does not have suitable low-cost index funds, invest up to the company match in the best low-cost fund available to get the "free money" and then open an IRA, which offers a much larger selection of low-cost funds with which you can complete your desired portfolio. Young investors should always take advantage of saving in their investment retirement account at a level that triggers the maximum "match" from their employer.

If you do not have a company retirement plan, consider an Individual Retirement Account (IRA). There are two main types: Traditional and Roth. Contributions to a Traditional IRA are deductible on your taxes but taxable when withdrawn. Contributions to a Roth IRA are not deductible, but withdrawals are tax free. If you expect to be in a higher tax bracket in retirement, and do not need the tax deduction now, it is usually better to choose the Roth. One advantage of a Roth IRA is that contributions may be withdrawn at any time without tax or penalty. Nearly all mutual fund companies (and banks) will be happy to open an IRA for you.

From the IRS Website, for 2017 Returns

Roth IRA and Traditional IRA annual contribution limits:

Age 49 and under = $5,500
Age 50 and older = $6,500

Traditional IRA modified adjusted gross income limit for partial deductibility:

Single = $62,000 up to $72,000
Married: Filing joint returns = $99,000 up to $119,000
Married: Filing separately = $0 up to $10,000
Non-active participant spouse = $186,000 up to $196,000

Roth IRA modified adjusted gross income phase-out ranges:

Single = $118,000 up to $133,000
Married: Filing joint returns = $186,000 up to $196,000
Married: Filing separately = $0 up to $10,000

Spousal IRAs: If you and your spouse file a joint return, the non-working spouse may be able to contribute to an IRA even if the other spouse did not. The amount of your combined contributions cannot be more than the taxable compensation reported on your joint return.

IRAs can be complicated, but for most of us it boils down to a decision whether to use a Traditional IRA or a Roth IRA. This is a general rule:

- **Use a Traditional IRA** if you think your income tax rate is *higher* now than it will be in retirement.
- **Use a Roth IRA** if you think your income tax rate is *lower* now than it will be in retirement.

If you want more detailed information, use this link to the IRS website: "Individual Retirement Arrangements (IRAs)":

https://www.irs.gov/retirement-plans/individual-retirement-arrangements-iras-1

If you are not eligible for a tax-advantaged retirement plan because you have no earned income, or if you have maxed out your retirement plan(s), or if for some other reason you are not eligible, don't despair. A low-cost, broad-market equity index fund or an ETF is very tax efficient. A taxable account has the advantage of *liquidity.* You may take your money out anytime, for any reason (although capital gains taxes may be due).

There is one overriding rule when selecting funds or ETFs for taxable accounts: *In taxable accounts, use only tax-efficient funds.* This is because, if you later sell or exchange a taxable fund that is profitable, it usually triggers a capital gains tax. Total Stock Market and Total International Stock Market funds are excellent tax-efficient funds for taxable accounts when tax-advantaged accounts are full or unavailable.

The Total Bond Market Fund is not tax-efficient and should normally be placed in a tax-advantaged account. If you don't have space for all of your bonds in your tax-advantaged accounts, consider a high quality tax-exempt intermediate-term bond fund, such as Vanguard's Tax-Exempt Intermediate-Term Bond Fund (VWIUX), for your taxable account. And, if you are in a higher tax bracket and live in a state with an income tax, a state-specific tax-free bond fund should also be considered for your taxable account.

Morningstar has a free Tax-Equivalent Yield Calculator to help you determine whether to use a taxable or tax-exempt bond fund:

www.screen.morningstar.com/BondCalc/BondCalculator_TaxEquivalent.html

In a nutshell, here is my advice on fund placement for maximum tax efficiency: Place the Total Bond Market Fund in tax-advantaged account(s). If full, use a tax-exempt bond fund in a taxable account. Place the Total Stock Market and the Total International Stock Market Funds in either a tax-advantaged account (best) or a taxable account.

Your fifth step is implementing your plan.

Let's review:

Step 1: You have selected three total market index funds or substitute funds.

Step 2: You have determined your all-important asset-allocation plan.

Step 3: You have decided whether to use mutual funds or ETFs.

Step 4: You have selected the best *type* of account(s).

Step 5: Now it is time to implement your plan.

At the time of writing, Fidelity and Schwab are in a low-cost bidding war with Vanguard. The result is that a select few of their total market index funds are as cheap or cheaper than Vanguard (by 0.01%). Assuming Fidelity and Schwab maintain very low expense ratios (ERs) in their total market index funds, this is good news for investors. (Be sure to check the fine print, to be certain that what appears in an ad is not just a single "loss leader" designed to bring you in as a client.)

I suggest that you consider Fidelity, Schwab, or Vanguard or any other company offering total market index funds with low expense ratios. A few basis points (a "basis point" is 1/100 of one percent) is less important than a company's strength, reputation and service. Simply contact the company for instructions on how to get started with your new target fund or The Three-Fund Portfolio:

CONTACT INFORMATION

Company	Website	Telephone
Fidelity	www.fidelity.com	800-343-3548
Schwab	www.schwab.com	800-435-4000
Vanguard	www.vanguard.com	877-662-7447

If your current securities are in a tax-advantaged account, you should be able to exchange your existing portfolio for a Three-Fund Portfolio without any tax consequences.

If your current securities are in a taxable account, and if they're profitable, you need to consider any resulting taxes and fees before selling existing securities. This is a common problem and is the reason it is so important for investors to use tax-efficient funds when investing in taxable accounts. Here are five steps to minimize taxes:

1. Stop making contributions into unwanted and tax-inefficient securities.
2. Stop reinvesting distributions.
3. Determine the amount of gain or loss in each taxable security.
4. If any security has a loss, consider selling and taking the tax-loss benefit.
5. If any security has a profit, consider selling up to the amount of your losses (after being held for one year to benefit from the lower capital gains tax rate).

Numbers 4 and 5 will be a wash and will result in zero tax. Put the proceeds from your sales into the appropriate tax-efficient total market index fund(s).

Before selling your remaining securities, you have a decision to make: whether to continue holding the tax-inefficient securities you don't want, or bite the bullet, pay the tax and begin to enjoy a less-costly, simpler, more tax-efficient portfolio using total market index funds.

Caveat: Older investors should keep in mind that under the 2018 federal law, the estate and gift tax exemption is $5.60 million per individual (double for spouses filing a joint return). For this reason, elderly or sickly investors should avoid selling securities with large capital gains, because taxes on the sale of these securities, after death, will be eliminated.

Once you have decided to sell unwanted securities, you must then consider the type of account in which to place your new holdings. If possible, it is almost always better to place your entire Three-Fund Portfolio in tax-advantaged accounts (except for short-term cash needs). However, if your 401k, 403b, IRA or other tax-advantaged accounts have been funded to the legal limit, you *must* then utilize a taxable account.

If you have questions on fund placement that I have not answered, please post them on the Bogleheads forum at www.bogleheads. org, where amateur and professional Bogleheads will be happy to help you.

Bogleheads Speak Out

"Hi, since 2009, I have stayed the course and ignored the noise with 'The Three-Fund Portfolio.' Results so far: One happy bogle-bot. I'm so glad I joined this forum after reading your book."

—RO

"I went with a three-fund portfolio in my HSA—so simple, so effective, so peaceful."

—GV

"As I got a little older, I learned the value of simplicity and now am a happy 3-funder. Adjusting to Admiral and 3-fund cut my expense ratio by over 0.5% and my portfolio is performing very well."

—MC

"It takes a well-educated intelligent person to come up with the simple 3-fund portfolio."

—QW

Costs Matter and They Are Coming Down (Thank You, Jack)

When widely respected columnist Jonathan Clements speaks, it pays to listen. As Mr. Bogle frequently points out, costs are the number one determinant of long-term investment performance. The more you save by avoiding costs, the more you keep. Clements tells readers they can build a great portfolio for next to nothing. The price war between Fidelity and Schwab, both competing against Vanguard, may come to an end, but Clements says it's unlikely that things will change at Vanguard, "which aims to operate each fund at cost." Remember that, the next time you compare investing in The Three-Fund Portfolio with investing in more expensive alternatives. What you save when you invest with Vanguard ends up in your pocket, not in someone else's.

Source: Jonathan Clements, "Next to Nothing," *Humble Dollar*, April 8, 2017, http://www.humbledollar.com/2017/04/next-to-nothing/

------ ◆ ------

CHAPTER SIX

Stay the Course

I f you have followed the five steps in the previous chapter, you are well on your way to meeting your investment goals. You must stay the course you have chosen, but it won't always be easy. You will be confronted with many temptations to make changes. Here are two that you must resist:

Bull Markets: When stocks are in a Bull Market, there will be a great temptation to increase your stock allocation. A small deviation from your asset allocation plan is permissible, but you should rebalance any time your stock allocation exceeds 10% (some would say 5%) of its desired allocation. If you are in the *accumulation phase* of investing, you can do this by putting all new contributions into your bond fund or by selling stocks. If you are in the *withdrawal phase* of investing, you should take withdrawals from your stock funds, or exchange stocks for additional bonds in your tax-advantaged account(s).

Bear Markets: When stocks are in a Bear Market (U.S., International, or both), you will be strongly tempted to sell at least a portion of your stock funds. DON'T DO IT. This is the time when stocks are on sale at lower prices. Sticking with your allocation means you likely will be buying low and selling high when you rebalance—the opposite direction of the herd. Rebalance by adding to your stock funds until you have again met your desired asset allocation. This is the most difficult (but most important) thing you can do in a Bear Market. Here is what Jack Bogle wrote in his classic, *Common Sense on Mutual Funds.*

> **Stay the course.** No matter what happens, stick to your program. I've said, 'Stay the course' a thousand times, and I meant it every time. *It's the most important single piece of investment wisdom I can give to you.*

It takes knowledge and willpower to stay the course and avoid succumbing to carefully prepared (and often misleading) marketing by mutual funds, insurance companies, banks, advisors and others seeking to make a profit from your investments. However, millions have now discovered the wisdom in Jack Bogle's advice and are following it.

Bogleheads Speak Out

"We're using the Three-Fund Portfolio across the board. I wish I could convey how much I appreciate what you've done."

—RE

"Don't let the trivia distract you. I've been down that road before and now ended up with my own three-fund portfolio."

—MU

"I moved everything to Taylor's 3-fund portfolio. I am a happy camper!"

—JA

"The venerable Three-Fund Portfolio is a marvelously simple and effective way to invest."

—PI

College Endowments Compared with The Three-Fund Portfolio

Each year, the National Association of College and University Business Officers (NACUBO) issues a Commonfund Study of Endowments (NCSE). This is a much-anticipated study, because colleges and universities are highly competitive. The schools have access to the best stock and bond fund managers and use the largest and best-connected groups of advisors and consultants—the finest money can buy. Investments include venture capital, real estate, timber, hedge funds, and derivatives, among others, and we would expect these endowments to outperform most individual investors.

Ben Carlson, CFA, writes for the newsletter, *A Wealth of Common Sense*. In his February 2018 column, "How the Bogle Model Beats the Yale Model," he compared the 2017 investment returns of the Vanguard Three-Fund Portfolio with the average returns of the 809 U.S. college and university endowments reported in the NCSE study. Here are the results:

Endowments	1 Year	3 Years	5 Years	10 Years
The Three-Fund Portfolio	14.9%	5.6%	10.3%	5.5%
Average Endowment Return	12.2%	4.2%	7.9%	4.6%

APPENDIX I

What Experts Say

American Association of Individual Investors: "It should come as no surprise that behavioral finance research makes a strong case for buying and holding low-cost, broadly-diversified index funds."

Mark Balasa, CPA, CFP: "That three-pronged approach is going to beat the vast majority of the individual stock and bond portfolio—that most people have at brokerage firms. There is a certain elegance in the simplicity of it."

Christine Benz, Morningstar Director of Personal Finance: "It's hard to find fault with the 'three-fund portfolio' espoused by many Bogleheads."

Bill Bernstein, author of *The Four Pillars of Investing*: "Does this [Three-Fund] portfolio seem overly simplistic, even amateurish? Get over it. Over the next few decades, the overwhelming majority of all professional investors will not be able to beat it."

Jack Bogle: "The beauty of owning the market is that you eliminate individual stock risk, you eliminate market sector risk, and you eliminate manager risk"; and from his *Common Sense on Mutual Funds*, "There may be better investment strategies than owning just three broad-based index funds but the number of strategies that are worse is infinite."

Scott Burns, financial columnist: "The odds are really, really poor that any of us will do better than a low-cost broad index fund."

Jonathan Burton, MarketWatch: "There are plenty of ways to complicate investing, and plenty of people who stand to make money from you as a result. So just think of a three-fund strategy as something you won't have to think about too much."

Andrew Clarke, co-author of *Wealth of Experience*: "If your stock portfolio looks very different from the broad stock market, you're assuming additional risk that may, or may not, pay off."

Jonathan Clements, author and *Wall Street Journal* columnist: "Using broad-based index funds to match the market is, I believe, brilliant in its simplicity."

John Cochrane, President, American Finance Association: "The market in aggregate always gets the allocation of capital right."

***Consumer Reports Money Book*:** "Simply buy the market as a whole."

Aswath Damodaran, Professor at New York University and author of more than 20 finance books: "Beating the market is never easy and anyone who argues otherwise is fighting history and ignoring the evidence."

Phil DeMuth, author of *The Affluent Investor*: "Buying and holding a few broad market index funds is perhaps the most important move ordinary investors can make to supercharge their portfolios."

Laura Dogu, U.S. Ambassador to Nicaragua and co-author of *The Bogleheads' Guide to Retirement Planning*: "With only these three funds in your investment portfolio you can benefit from low costs and broad diversification and still have a portfolio that is easy to manage."

Charles Ellis, author of *Winning the Loser's Game*: "The stock market is clearly too efficient for most of us to do better."

Eugene Fama, Nobel Laureate: "For most people, the market portfolio is the most sensible decision."

Rick Ferri, *Forbes* columnist and author of six investment books: "The older I get, the more I believe the 3-fund portfolio is an excellent choice for most people. It's simple, cheap, easy to maintain, and has no tracking error that would cause emotional abandonment to the strategy."

Mark Hulbert, *Hulbert Financial Digest*: "Buying and holding a broad-market index fund remains the best course of action for most investors."

Sheldon Jacobs, author of *Guide to Successful No-Load Fund Investing*: "The best index fund for almost everyone is the Total Stock Market Index Fund. The fund can only go wrong if the market goes down and never comes back again, which is not going to happen."

***Kiplinger's Retirement Report*:** "You'll beat most investors with just three funds that cover the vast majority of global stock and bond markets: Vanguard Total Stock Market; Vanguard Total International Stock Index and Vanguard Total Bond Market Index."

Lawrence Kudlow, CNBC: "I like the concept of the Wilshire 5000, which essentially gives you a piece of the rock of all actively-traded companies."

Professor Burton Malkiel, author of *A Random Walk Down Wall Street*: "I recommend a total market index fund—one that follows the entire U.S. stock market. And I recommend the same approach for the U.S. bond market and international stocks."

Harry Markowitz, Nobel Laureate: "A foolish attempt to beat the market and get rich quickly will make one's broker rich and oneself much less so."

Bill Miller, famed fund manager: "With the market beating 91% of surviving managers since the beginning of 1982, it looks pretty efficient to me."

E. F. Moody, author of *No Nonsense Finance*: "I am increasingly convinced that the best investment advice for both individual and institutional equity investors is to buy a low-cost broad-based index fund that holds all the stocks comprising the market portfolio."

The Motley Fool: "Invest your long-term moolah in index mutual funds that are designed to track the performance of a broad market index."

John Norstad, mathematician: "For total market investors, the three disciplines of history, arithmetic, and reason all say that they will succeed in the end."

Anna Prior, *Wall Street Journal* writer: "A simple portfolio of 3 funds. It may sound counter-intuitive, but for the average individual investor, less is actually more."

Jane Bryant Quinn, syndicated columnist and author of *Making the Most of Your Money*: "The dependable great investment returns come from index funds which invest in the stock market as a whole."

Pat Regnier, former Morningstar analyst: "We should just forget about choosing fund managers and settle for index funds to mimic the market."

Ron Ross, author of *The Unbeatable Market*: "Giving up the futile pursuit of beating the market is the surest way to increase your investment efficiency and enhance your financial peace of mind."

Allan Roth, CPA, CFP, financial advisor and author of *How a Second Grader Beat Wall Street*: "The beauty of a 3-fund portfolio is that it automatically builds the global portfolio without having to worry about standard deviations, correlations, Sharpe ratios, and the like."

Paul Samuelson, Nobel Laureate: "The most efficient way to diversify a stock portfolio is with a low-fee index fund. Statistically, a broadly-based stock index fund will outperform most actively-managed equity portfolios."

Bill Schultheis, author of *The Coffeehouse Investor*: "You don't need to have eight funds. You can do it with two or three and have a great portfolio."

Chandan Sengupta, author of *The Only Proven Road to Investment Success*: "Use a low-cost, broad-based index fund to passively invest in a little bit of a large number of stocks."

Prof. Jeremy Siegel, author of *Stocks for the Long Run*: "For most of us, trying to beat the market leads to disastrous results."

Dan Solin, author of *The Smartest Portfolio You'll Ever Own*: "You can get as simple or as complicated as you'd like. You can keep it very simple by owning just three mutual funds that invest in domestic stocks, foreign stocks, and bonds. That's precisely what I recommend in my model portfolios."

William Spitz, author of *Get Rich Slowly*: "Few are able to beat a simple strategy of buying and holding the securities that comprise the market."

Professor Meir Statman, author of *What Investors Really Want*: "It makes sense to have those three funds. What makes it hard is that it seems too simple to actually be a winner."

Robert Stovall, investment manager: "It's just not true that you can't beat the market. Every year about one-third do it. Of course, each year it is a different group."

Peter D. Teresa, Morningstar Senior Analyst: "My recommendation: A fund that indexes the entire market, such as Vanguard Total Stock Market Index."

Kent Thune, CFP, editor of *The Financial Philosopher*: "In keeping with the virtues of passive investing, combined with Bogle's haystack philosophy, we can capture the entire market of securities with Vanguard index funds, investing in just three broad categories: U.S. stocks, foreign stocks and bonds."

Walter Updegrave, author and senior editor of *Money* magazine: "Simply invest in the following three funds (or their ETF equivalents): a total U.S. stock market fund, a total international stock market fund and a total U.S bond market fund. Do that, and you'll gain exposure to virtually every type of publicly-traded stock in the world (large and small, growth and value, domestic and foreign, all industries and sectors), as well as the entire U.S. investment-grade taxable bond market (short- to-long-term maturities, corporates, Treasuries and mortgage-backed issues)."

Wilshire Associates: "The market portfolio offers the best ratio of return to risk."

Jason Zweig, *Wall Street Journal*'s finance columnist, commenting on the Benjamin Graham classic, *The Intelligent Investor*: "The single best choice for a lifelong holding is a total stock-market index fund."

Meet the Bogleheads

Mel Lindauer, President, The John C. Bogle Center for Financial Literacy

EARLY HISTORY

In 1998, there was an effort by Taylor Larimore and others to create a new online discussion forum at Morningstar.com. The new forum would be devoted to discussions of index fund investing as espoused by Vanguard founder, John C. (Jack) Bogle. The folks leading this effort were called "Bogleheads." Back then, the term "Bogleheads" was used by non-Bogleheads as a bit of a derogatory term. However, we Bogleheads accepted it as a badge of honor.

Morningstar finally gave in to the pressure and established the new forum, but they were reluctant to name it the "Bogleheads" because they were concerned that it might be considered offensive. Instead, they chose to name the new forum the "Vanguard Diehards," with a subheading "Bogleheads Unite to Talk About Your Favorite Fund Company."

The new forum was a smashing success and soon became the most popular forum on Morningstar.com. Eventually, the number of posts on the new forum surpassed the count of all the other Morningstar forums combined.

BOGLEHEAD CONFERENCES

Jack Bogle responded to a Thanksgiving 1999 post he saw on the forum, asking if there were any interest in getting together with him for a day at a non-resort location. Of course there was, so Taylor and I decided to have our first-ever Boglehead get-together with Jack in Miami, where he was to be the keynote speaker at the 2001 *Miami Herald* Making Money seminar. That event, held in Taylor and Pat's bayside condominium, turned into an almost-annual conference with Jack Bogle as the guest of honor. Subsequent events were held in Philadelphia, Chicago, Denver, Las Vegas, Washington, D.C., San Diego, and Dallas/Ft. Worth.

Because of concerns about his health, we decided to minimize Jack's travel, so we've held all subsequent events in Philadelphia. The 2017 Bogleheads Conference was the sixteenth in the series. (We missed one year when we were writing our first book, *The Bogleheads' Guide to Investing.*)

THE BIG MOVE

In 2007, the Bogleheads moved from Morningstar and formed our own forum at www.Bogleheads.org. Born out of frustration over the lack of moderating and the difficulties with the website at Morningstar, the new, moderated Bogleheads.org forum has been a remarkable success. Today, the new forum has become the premier investing forum on the Internet.

FORUM STATISTICS

As of this writing, the new forum is getting up to 4.5 million hits per day and is visited by as many as 90,000 unique individuals daily. While individuals must register to post (it's free), registration is not required to read the millions of previously-posted questions and answers. (This is affectionately known as "lurking").

There are more than 70,000 registered Boglehead members from around the globe. At any one time, there are between 1,000 and 2,000 individuals online. Of that number, unregistered guests (the lurkers) normally outnumber registered members by approximately 10 to 1. Projecting that figure could mean that as many as 700,000 or more investors visit the forum from time to time.

Registered members have made more than 3,700,000 posts on more than 227,000 topics.

While all this is certainly impressive, what really makes the Boglehead community so very special is the *quality* of both the help and the information offered by so many selfless Bogleheads, who want to contribute in any way they can to help our community help others reach their financial goals.

LOCAL CHAPTERS

At the time of this writing, there are 73 local Bogleheads chapters throughout the United States and 6 foreign chapters (Paris, Taiwan, Singapore, Hong Kong, UAE/Dubai, and Israel). Chapter leaders communicate with their members using the Local Chapters and Bogleheads Community subsection of the Bogleheads.org forum. There, they establish meeting dates, times, locations, agendas, and any other issues of importance. Here's a rather lengthy link to the Google map showing locations of Bogleheads local chapters, along with contact information: https://www.google.com/maps/d/u/0/viewer?mid=1KX-WSvjOwmi1fLocIrz5wHiBB7s&ll=36.70875191 9221015%2C-95.86343664218749&z=3.

WIKI

Our community's wiki is the repository of a wealth of investing information, contributed by nearly 250 Boglehead editors who want to help other investors gain financial literacy. There are currently more than 900 pages of content covering a multitude of investing topics such as asset allocation, taxes, rebalancing and a host of other important subjects, all written and kept updated by those Boglehead editors. Our wiki editors continue to add important information on an ongoing basis. The wiki averages about 25,000 visits per day, but there have been days when that number approached 35,000. For those who feel overwhelmed, the wiki offers a "Getting Started" section. There's a link to the wiki on nearly every page of the Bogleheads.org forum.

BOGLEHEADS BOOKS

The Bogleheads' message has been expanded even further by the publication of two previous Bogleheads books—*The Bogleheads' Guide to Investing* and *The Bogleheads' Guide to Retirement Planning*. *The Bogleheads' Guide to The Three-Fund Portfolio* is the third in the series. We have a number of published investment authors who freely contribute their knowledge to the forum on a regular basis. Even Vanguard founder, Jack Bogle, posts on the forum from time to time.

THE JOHN C. BOGLE CENTER FOR FINANCIAL LITERACY

The John C. Bogle Center for Financial Literacy was established in 2010 and is an IRS-approved 501(c)(3) charitable organization. The Center was established to continue Vanguard founder John C. Bogle's crusade to see that investors get their fair share of market returns and to raise the level of financial literacy for all investors so they may realize their goals and achieve financial independence.

Second, the Bogle Center has helped with the funding of the www.bogleheads.org online investing forum, that works to educate investors from around the world. The forum is now the world's largest commercial-free financial forum on the Internet.

The Bogle Center organizes and manages the annual Bogleheads conferences that educate investors from around the country and around the world. Our conferences have attracted attendees from nearly every state in the union, as well as attendees from several foreign countries. The conferences are a great success and are usually sold out within a few days following their announcement.

The Bogle Center works to educate the public about sound financial principles, including living below one's means; staying out of debt; saving; investing wisely in a diversified, tax-efficient manner; minimizing investment costs; and contributing to available tax-advantaged plans to help them reach their financial goals.

Taylor is graciously donating all royalties from this book to the Bogle Center. If you would like to join him in Jack's crusade "to give ordinary investors a fair shake," please mail your tax-deductible donation to:

> The John C. Bogle Center for Financial Literacy
> 6977 Navajo Road, Suite 147
> San Diego, CA 92119-1503

Glossary of Financial Terms

Active management: An investment strategy that seeks to outperform the returns of the financial markets or a particular benchmark

Annualize: To make a period of less than a year apply to a full year. For example, a six-month return of 5 percent would be *annualized* at 10 percent.

Automatic reinvestment: An arrangement whereby mutual fund distributions (dividends and capital gains) are used to buy additional shares

Benchmark index: An index used by a mutual fund manager to compare against his or her fund's performance

Bond duration: Provides an estimate of a bond fund's volatility. For example, a bond fund with a three-year duration will decrease in value by approximately 3 percent if interest rates rise 1 percent, while a bond fund with a five-year duration will decrease in value by approximately 5 percent if interest rates rise by the same 1 percent.

Capital gain: The difference between the purchase price and the sale price

Capital gain distribution: Payments to mutual fund shareholders of gains on the net sale of securities in the fund

Equities: Stocks

Exchange-traded fund (ETF): An index fund that trades on the stock market. ETFs are purchased and sold through a broker.

Expense ratio: The percentage of a fund's net assets used to pay a portion of its annual expenses

Extended Market Index Fund: A fund of about 3,000 broadly based stocks that, when combined with an S&P 500 Index Fund in an approximate 1:5 ratio, is nearly identical to a total market index fund

Index fund: A type of mutual fund constructed to include all or most of the components of a given market sector

Long-term capital gain: Profit on the sale of a security held at least one year, that generally results in a lower tax

Market timing: Attempting to forecast market direction and then investing based on the forecasts

Price/earnings ratio (P/E): A stock's current price divided by its earnings

Reversion to the Mean: The theory that prices and returns eventually will tend to move to the average price over time

Risk tolerance: The investor's ability to endure declines in the value of investments without selling and without worry—often called your "sleep well at night factor."

Rollover: A tax-free transfer of assets from one retirement plan to another

Roth IRA: A tax-favored retirement plan. Contributions are not deductible, but earnings are tax-free during accumulation and also when withdrawn.

Target Retirement fund: A mutual fund comprised of a portfolio of mutual funds that becomes more conservative with age

Taxable account: An account in which the securities are subject to annual federal taxes

Tax advantaged: Any type of investment, account, or plan that is exempt from taxation, is tax deferred, or offers other types of tax benefits (IRAs, 401Ks, and municipal bonds are examples.)

Tax-deferred account: An account in which federal income taxes are deferred until withdrawn

Tax efficient: Owing the least amount in taxes

Tax inefficient: Owing more tax than necessary

Tax-loss harvesting: The practice of selling a taxable security with a loss to offset other taxable income and gains

Total Market Index Fund: A mutual fund or exchange-traded fund (ETF) composed of nearly all the investable companies in all market sectors

Traditional IRA: A tax-favored retirement plan. Contributions are deductible and the tax on both the contributions and earnings are deferred during accumulation. Withdrawals are taxed at one's ordinary income tax rates. Penalties apply if withdrawals are made prior to age 59-1/2 except in limited situations.

Turnover rate: An indication of the manager's trading activity during the past year

Unrealized capital gain/loss: A gain or loss that would be realized if the fund's securities were sold

Index